Taxation Is Theft

How politicians force us to fund our own abuse —and what we can do about it

Elliot "Alu" Axelman

Also by Alu

The Blueprint For Liberty
Articles of Secession
The Plague That Must Not Be Questioned
The Progressive Solution
Presumed Guilty
They Fear Unity
How Amazing Is The U.S. Constitution?
The Pocket Guide to Killing Gun Control

Foreword

On February 27th, 2016, I posted a meme to a Facebook page I moderated named "Anarchyball." The meme was titled, "Seven things every child needs to hear." Those seven things were:

1. I love you
2. I'm proud of you
3. I'm sorry
4. I forgive you
5. I'm listening
6. Taxation is theft
7. You've got what it takes

You've probably noticed that number six sticks out. It takes you by surprise. It causes a reaction. And the reaction from my post that day led to over 5,000 shares of the meme, kick-starting a cultural phenomenon of people en masse questioning taxation. In the process of this awakening, people asked, "But who will build the roads?" and "But what about national defense?" Others angrily commented, "Do you just want children to starve?" and "You must hate America!"

Thousands of comments and debates later, many started to recognize that the U.S. government doesn't really use taxation in all the benign, idealized ways people default to talking about, such as paying for roads, courts, and police. The U.S. government spends a significant amount of taxation on perpetual wars abroad, putting people into jail over victimless crimes, and on bailing out crony corporations that bankroll politicians year after year. The U.S. debt as of this writing totals over $31 trillion, of which about 25 trillion has been added in just the last 20 years. This is more than the annual gross domestic product for the entire union. Simply put: it's unsustainable.

But communicating the specifics of why taxation is unsustainable is no easy task, as it involves going through several key ideas in philosophy, economics, ethics, and finance. Fortunately, Alu Axelman has put together this book to lay out precisely how and why taxation is theft, with robust detail on how the government's monopoly on force is used to expand its empire and erode the wealth of everyday Americans. His coverage of various taxes, their uses, and effects, puts into clear context why taxation requires more than just reformation. It requires abolition. It requires supplanting taxation with a new model that only accepts voluntary contributions as an ultimate check against state power.

Even if you're new to these ideas, Alu makes it accessible for anyone to dive into and understand. I hope you enjoy this read as much as I have in being reminded of the many ways we are stolen from by the state and how those in the state use our own resources against us.

Cheers to a freer future as we make this journey together and strive toward voluntary solutions.

In liberty,

-Jack V Lloyd, J.D.

Note

You will find that I have purposely used lowercase letters for the "united states" throughout this book. There is a reason why I do not capitalize those two words.

After years of being a pro-America patriot who believed that we all could and should unite under one set of values, I have come to realize that each of the 50 states is unique and ought to be independently governed. No two states have the same cultures. New Hampshire, California, Texas, New Jersey, Wyoming, and Georgia are all quite different from one another, aren't they?

By capitalizing "United states" or by referring to it as "USA," "America," or as "one country," you are reinforcing the idea that we are all citizens of one nation, meaning we all have the same value system. That is not the case.

Chapter 1: The History of Taxation

In the 18th century, the American colonists separated from Britain. In the 19th century, slavery was outlawed. In the 20th century, women were granted the right to vote. In the 21st century, could mandatory taxation be abolished?

In the 1770s, the colonists revolted against the greatest empire in the world, knowing that they faced certain death if they failed in this violent act of treason. But they could no longer stand by and absorb the 'long train of abuses' by the far-away tyrants who ruled over them. Perhaps the most severe abuse that the founders sought to escape was the extortion that King George used in order to steal their money. The extortion (also referred to by statists as 'taxation') amounted to very little[1] of each individual's total annual income.

In 1638, the Massachusetts government required everyone to support both the state and the church. Direct taxation took two forms: a wealth tax and a poll tax. Based on an average income of 12 pounds per year, the Hoover Institution[2] calculates that the one-shilling poll-tax rate was an effective 0.4% annual income tax and that the annual wealth (property) tax had a rate of around 0.1–0.4%.

Even under the British government, there was no tax on income. One of the few major taxes was on windows. When the window tax[3] was introduced, it consisted of two parts: a flat-rate house tax of 2 shillings per house (equivalent to $17 in 2021) and a variable tax for the number of windows above ten windows. Properties with between ten and twenty windows paid a total of four shillings (comparable to $34 in 2021), and those with more than twenty windows paid eight shillings.

The British also imposed tariffs on imports of slaves, tobacco, and alcoholic beverages. In all, the average tariff worked out to about 10% of the value of imports. In 1764, Parliament passed the Sugar Act, imposing a tax of one penny per gallon on molasses imports, equivalent to around $2 per gallon today.

The British government also utilized simple extortion to steal real property from the colonists, an act so vicious that even American politicians would never ever do such a thing! (see Chapter 4: Current State of The Theft.) In 1772, a man from Weare, New Hampshire named Able Ebenezer Mudgett refused to allow the King's men to steal his trees to be used for their navy ships. When the police came to take his white pine trees, Ebenezer and his neighbors brutally beat the sheriff and his deputy,[4] including one strike for each log that was cut down and ordered to be seized by the government. They ran the cops out of town, and they didn't have any more problems with them in the future. The 'Pine Tree Riot' remains a large part of New Hampshire lore and is celebrated on April 13th each year.

Just a few years later, the Townshend Acts started making their way through the British government. One of the new laws imposed a tax on tea of four pence per pound ($8 today). In 1773, opposition to these taxes culminated in the Boston Tea Party,[5] a rebellious act that involved throwing

92,000 pounds of British tea into the harbor. The King considered it an act of treason.

The colonists were furious about the taxation and their lack of representation in the British Parliament. The Parliament was elected by British citizens and the Governors of each colony (State) were appointed by the King. The colonists were not adequately represented in the government of Britain, though some might argue that they hardly had less representation than we have in the federal government today. This will be discussed in detail in a later chapter.

In April 1775,[6] the first battles of the American Revolution began in the colony of Massachusetts.

On July 4th, 1776, the 13 colonies declared independence, telling the British King that they were seceding from his empire. The British went to war to keep the colonists under their control. In 1783, the war came to an end, and the 13 colonies officially completed their secession from Britain. Each colony became an independent state at peace, governing itself in every way. The states formed a Congress and began developing an agreement to form an alliance with each other. In 1777, the founders passed the Articles of Confederation, which was ratified by all 13 states by 1781. The Articles created a central government that was barely existent. It had no power to tax the people; it would be sustained by receiving money from the states within the union. Political leaders who desired a powerful central government successfully called a convention to amend the Articles a few years later.

In 1787, the 55 delegates[7] of the convention did not simply adjust the Articles of Confederation. They totally scrapped it and drafted a new Constitution, one which gave the federal government much more power, including the power to define its own limitations. The new Constitution also neglected to prescribe any punishment for government officials who violated the Constitution. The Constitution passed the convention once 41 delegates signed it. The new document was then sent to the state legislatures for ratification. On June 21, 1788, New Hampshire became the ninth state to ratify the Constitution, thereby causing the new document to go into effect.

President George Washington signed the Tariff Act of July 4, 1789, which authorized the collection of tariff duties (customs) on imported goods. By 1790, political leaders from all 13 states ratified the new Constitution, though many citizens strongly condemned[8] the document as anti-liberty. But the requisite number of politicians in each state voted to accept the new Constitution, so it became the law for everyone, including those who opposed it.

Many individuals believe that the Constitution was a terrible mistake[9] for liberty and that it greatly diminished personal freedom.

During the early 19th century, the federal government stole money from people only by way of excise taxes and tariffs. The Tariff Act of 1789 was the first major piece of legislation passed in the union after the ratification of the Constitution and it had two purposes: to protect manufacturing industries developing in the union and to raise revenue for the federal government. The act levied a 50¢ per ton duty on goods imported by foreign ships; American-owned vessels were charged 6¢ per ton. Congress also imposed low excise taxes on a few goods, such as whiskey, rum, tobacco, snuff, and refined sugar.

The first federal budget was about $4.6 million and the population in the 1790 Census was about 4,000,000, so the average total federal tax burden was about $1 per person per year. At that time, tradesmen earned about $0.25 a day, so federal taxes could be paid with about four days' work. Paying even this was usually optional, as taxed imports listed on the tariff lists could usually be avoided by buying domestic products if desired.

The whiskey excise tax collected so little and was so despised that it was abolished by President Thomas Jefferson in 1802.

In 1861, Abraham Lincoln signed a bill into law that created a federal income tax[10] for the first time. The Revenue Act imposed a 3% tax on annual incomes over $800 ($24,000 in 2022's dollars). Congress repealed the tax once the war ended. After the Civil War, Congress once again focused its taxation efforts on tobacco and alcohol. Congress repealed the income tax in 1872 and then restored it in 1894. In 1895, the SCOTUS ruled the income tax to be unconstitutional[11].

Lysander Spooner said in 1870 that the Constitution "has either authorized such a government as we have had, or has been powerless to prevent it."

In 1909, Congress passed the 16th Amendment, which created the federal income tax. It was ratified in 1913 by 42 state legislatures, officially adding to the U.S. Constitution that "The Congress shall have power to lay and collect taxes on incomes, from whatever source derived, without apportionment among the several states, and without regard to any census or enumeration."

Of course, the D.C. politicians sold the tax by convincing the people that it was only 1%-7%. The tax already had many of the sleazy features of the modern system. The tax was passed so easily because politicians exempted the first $3,000 for each individual, plus an additional $1,000 for married couples. This caused the tax to initially apply to less than 4% of the population, making it popular among everyone except for the ultra-wealthy. The new tax also created the powerful behavioral control system that politicians still utilize to this very day. The 1913 law used governmental policy to incentivize people to get married. Because of the higher percentages that applied to those with higher incomes, the new law also encouraged people to earn as little money as possible (on the books, at least). Today, the Lords of D.C. use the tax code to control behavior in countless ways, from encouraging people to buy solar panels[12] to rewarding people for having babies.[13]

Interestingly, the Federal Reserve Act was also passed into law by D.C. politicians in 1913. This legislation created a special bank that could loan money to the government by printing it on paper. Until this point, paper money represented real money (gold or silver) and was redeemable at the bank for real physical money. That began to change in

1913 when the politicians and the major banks colluded to create the Federal Reserve, a bank that was not accountable to the voters or to market forces. This bank is run by board members who are appointed by the President, they control interest rates for the united states, and they loan money to banks and to the government itself. The bank also controls the economy by buying or selling large amounts of assets,[14] thereby affecting the supply of products in the market. As of this writing, the Fed's assets total over $238 billion.[15]

Most states also tax the income earned by their residents. Wisconsin was the first to impose this productivity tax in 1911. Today, every state in the union besides New Hampshire, Florida, Wyoming, Alaska, Texas, South Dakota, Washington, Nevada, and Tennessee extorts additional money from the income of their residents. Additionally, states like New York, New Jersey, and California have local income taxes on top of their state taxes. In New York City, the 4% income tax was added to the 9% state income tax, which was added to my effective federal income tax of 22%. Add all of the other taxes like sales taxes and tolls, and roughly half of my annual income was being stolen by politicians until I moved to New Hampshire in 2017 to join the Free State Project.[16]

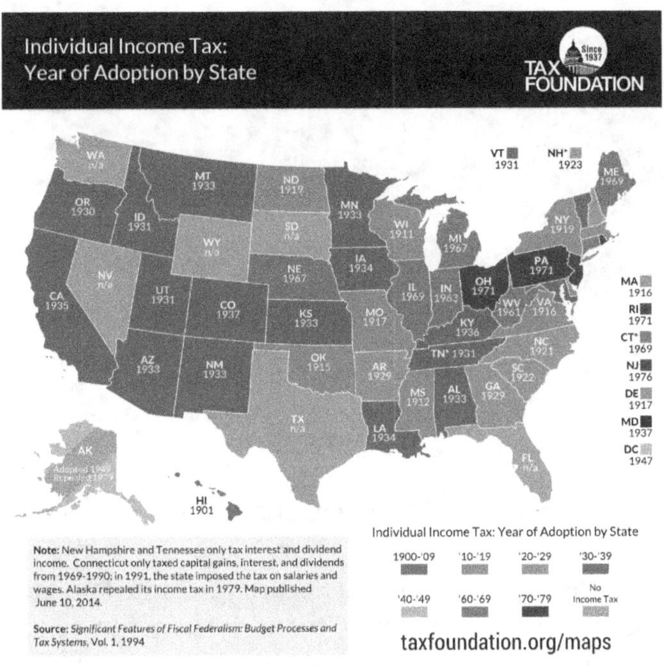

The next major event took place in 1933 when FDR confiscated all gold coins, bullion, and certificates from citizens and made it a crime to own gold. It would remain illegal to own gold until 1974. The federal government then declared that the price of gold was $35/ounce, up from $20. This relatively high price discouraged (naive) citizens from buying gold, allowing D.C. politicians to hoard the precious metal more easily. The high amount of Federal Reserve Notes (FRNs) each gold ounce was worth also increased the flow of gold from foreign governments to the federal government because other countries still valued the dollars more than gold when they could get $35 for each ounce.

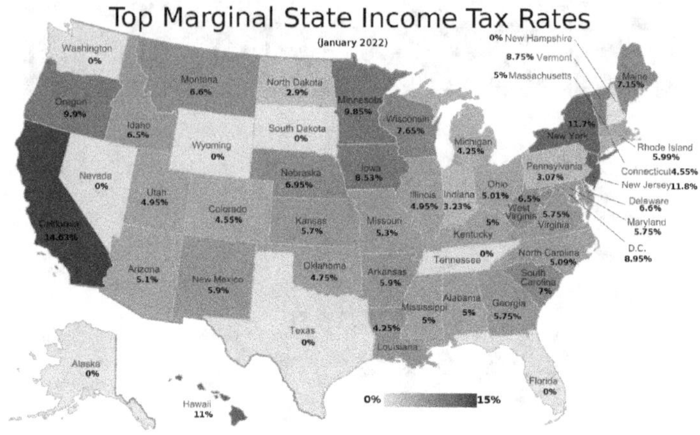

Still, in 1934, FRNs could be redeemed for silver.

In 1935, FDR signed the Social Security Act into law, creating a program that would pay monthly benefits to retired workers starting at age 65 or older. Of course, FDR and the greedy socialists in Congress knew when they created the program that the life expectancy for people born in 1935 was only 60.7 years.[17] The D.C. Empire planned to begin making SS payments to retirees over the age of 65 in 1940. Evil politicians like FDR knew that those born in 1880 had a life expectancy from birth of only 39 years. Some might surmise from this data that FDR didn't actually intend to pay back the stolen money to very many retirees.

Unfortunately for the politicians and despite their best efforts to suppress[18] effective medical care and innovation,[19] the life expectancy increased steadily until it began to flatten out at around 78 years in 2010. Politicians would have loved to raise the Social Security retirement age to 100 so that very few people could receive their stolen money back, but such a policy has proven to be very difficult for two big reasons: 1) the elderly are the most prolific voters, and 2) harming the elderly is political suicide due to being seen as a heartless act. Still, D.C. politicians have managed to increase the age from 65 to 67, and they are incentivizing[20] citizens to delay their retirement until the age of 70. I would not be shocked if they snuck a provision into a large bill that increases the age to 90 or 100 years sometime soon.

The act also established a payroll tax to fund the program and required employers to withhold the tax from employee wages. The original Social Security contribution rate was 1% of pay, which was matched by employers. At only 1%, it was easy enough for the people to digest without revolting. The tax rate grew to 1.5% in 1950 and gradually increased to 5% by 1978. The current Social Security tax rate of 6.2%[21] has been in effect since 1990. Whenever Joe Employer pays Tommy Worker $1,000, Joe and Tommy must each give $62.50 to D.C. politicians to comply with the payroll tax (Joe) and income tax (Tommy) that fund Social Security. The real Social Security tax is 12.4%; it is just split between the employer and the employee. Individuals might finally see the fruits of their labor when they turn ~~65~~ ~~66~~ 67 years old, though inflation is likely to make their government-run retirement account worth practically nothing.

Once they finally receive a tiny portion of the money back after it was stolen throughout their careers, the workers learn some more great news. Because they technically *received* money (the Social Security check) in the mail, the

IRS expects their piece of the cake.[22] In 1983, President Reagan signed the Social Security Amendments into law. This made 50% of Social Security payments to retirees into taxable income, literally taxing the elderly on their taxes.[23]

The split funding mechanism of Social Security also applies to the Medicare tax, which was created by President Lyndon Johnson in 1965.[24] The employer and employee are each forced to sacrifice 1.45% of their income each week to fund the massive federal Medicare system, which provides health insurance to people over the age of 65 and to some younger people with chronic medical conditions. You can learn the basics of this program by reading the D.C. Empire's 128-page handbook[25] or by reading the infinite legislation and regulations outlining the complexities of the system. Additionally, the Centers for Medicaid & Medicare Services (CMS) has since grown into a $1.3 trillion[26] monstrosity. The goliath controls healthcare by controlling insurance reimbursement rates, allowing them to largely control the medical policies throughout the united states. Because a high percentage of patients now use Medicare or Medicaid[27] as their primary insurance, the Lords in D.C. can control healthcare by choosing which procedures and medications to pay healthcare providers for, and how much to pay them. During corona-fascism, CMS tilted the scales by paying hospitals extra money for declaring patients to have COVID, as I explained in my book, *The Plague That Must Not Be Questioned*.[28] When they do not support a particular intervention, the Lords can instruct CMS not to reimburse doctors for it, which essentially guarantees that few doctors would provide their patients with that intervention.

Earnings	rate	hours	this period	year to date
Regular	25.1600	40.00	1,006.40	17,712.64
Overtime	37.7400	20.00	754.80	6,566.78
BONUS			200.00	600.00
IFT Diff	4.0000	12.00	48.00	859.00
Retro Pay			94.35	94.35
Weekend Differ	25.1600	12.00	48.00	817.00
Weekend IFT	25.1600	12.00	96.00	1,632.00
Earned Time				603.84
Holiday 0.5				305.07
Gross Pay			**$2,247.55**	29,190.68

Deductions	Statutory		
	Federal Income Tax	-380.95	4,264.32
Total theft:	Social Security Tax	-139.35	1,809.82
$552.88	Medicare Tax	-32.58	423.26
	Net Pay	**$1,694.67**	
	Checking	-1,608.42	
	Savings	-86.25	
	Net Check	**$0.00**	

Back to the history lesson.

In 1943, Congress and FDR passed the Current Tax Payment Act. This made a change to the method of tax collection that will live in infamy for as long as humans walk the earth. The new law instructed employers to withhold all employees' income taxes and send the money to DC. Prior to 1943, each individual received their full paycheck and had to painstakingly send a large chunk of it to their masters. By hiding the tax from the sight of workers, the federal government instantly made the tax much less painful, paving the way for massive tax increases in the future.

By 1944, the D.C. Empire held more than 75% of the world's gold. This made it very powerful. At this time, nearly every major country agreed at the UN meeting in Bretton Woods, New Hampshire to a new financial system: instead of using gold as the world's primary currency, they would all tie their currencies to the U.S. Dollar. *"But don't worry, because the dollar will be tied to gold at $35 per ounce!"* the D.C. Empire assured the other nations. The D.C. politicians began printing much more paper money than they could back up with gold. And other countries began to notice.

In the '50s and '60s, the D.C. politicians printed massive amounts of paper money to fund the $168 billion ($1.7 trillion in today's money) cost of the Vietnam war. This caused horrific inflation in the money supply and increases in prices.

In 1963, the federal government removed the words *"shall be paid to the bearer on demand"* from Federal Reserve Notes (FRNs). In 1968, the D.C. politicians stopped allowing people to redeem FRNs for silver.

"Governments cannot create gold or silver out of thin air . . . but they can create dollars out of thin air!"

In 1965, the government removed the silver from dimes and quarters. Up until that point, the coins contained 90% silver. But the crooks in D.C. took all the silver out of them, determined not to let the peasants even touch any real money.

In August 1971, France's government collected its remaining gold from the D.C. Empire by exchanging its dollars for the precious metal, and the governments of nearly every other country followed suit. They knew that they wanted to hold more gold and fewer FRNs, especially before American inflation went through the roof.

Later that month, President Nixon declared that the federal government would stop redeeming FRNs for gold, ending the Bretton Woods agreement. This broke an international contract and destroyed the D.C. Empire's credibility among the governments of the world.

Immediately, the value of the dollar plummeted, because other nations and even Americans no longer valued it at its supposed price of 1/35th of an ounce of gold. After all, it was no longer redeemable for gold. This caused a catastrophic devaluation of the dollar throughout the 1970s. While Nixon was a corrupt tyrant for severing the link between gold and the dollar, there was some truth to his concern that other countries were converting their dollars to gold, which was their right. Eventually, the reckless printing of dollars by D.C. politicians caused too many dollars to be in circulation. And once too many foreign governments exercised their right to redeem their dollars for gold at the D.C. Empire's Treasury, the federal government had no choice but to stop allowing dollars to be redeemed for gold, because they barely had any physical gold left in their vaults.

The result? Items that cost $1 in 1971 now cost $7.[29]

By working hand in hand with the newly established Federal Reserve, D.C. politicians were able to create paper money that was more detached from real money (gold and silver) than ever before.

In 1982, the federal government removed nearly all of the copper from pennies,[30] which previously were 95% composed of the useful metal. Today, pennies contain only 2.5% copper and are mostly made of zinc.

In 2020, the federal government quietly lowered the reserve requirement for banks to zero,[31] which essentially meant that they could claim to have infinite FRNs in their customers' accounts without having any FRNs in their actual banks.

In 2021, the federal government announced that due to inflation, they will cease production of the penny in 2023. Producing each penny costs over two cents,[32] meaning that they literally lose money when they mint the one–cent coins.

Throughout corona-fascism, the D.C. politicians created 25% of all dollars in existence. The trillions of dollars created each year by D.C. further dilute the value of each dollar you thought was securely in your possession. Inflation allows politicians to tax you without ever touching you or your money. Those that use the D.C. Empire's money suffer when they print more of it. Those that own gold, silver, crypto, or anything of value are protected from inflation.

Increasingly, Americans are discovering that they need to acquire sound money before corrupt politicians use their Ponzi Scheme[33] to rob them of all their worth.

Why do politicians want to devalue their own currency?

The federal government loves to spend. They spend money on wars, which requires them to pay soldiers and buy billions of dollars worth of weapons, technology, and other materials. They also spend billions they don't have on welfare and other forms of bribery in order to win the votes of undecided naive voters. But they don't want to raise taxes by billions of dollars in order to afford the massive spending increases, because that is a guaranteed way to lose the next election. So, they pretend to 'borrow' the money from the federal reserve. In 2019, the D.C. politicians spent around 5 trillion and took in around 3.5 trillion from taxation. The difference is called the 'deficit', and it plunges D.C. further into debt, which is now over 31 trillion dollars. Of course, they could never pay back this debt, but they do need to at least pay the interest on the debt each month if they want to maintain any dignity among the world governments. Our politicians are not smart, but they do know that 31 trillion is a very big number. But they also know that as each dollar depreciates in value, debt denominated in dollars also decreases in value. If I owe you $100 today and I pay back that same $100 in 70 years, it'll be much easier because $100 will be the value of a few peanuts in seven decades. Thus, inflation benefits debtors. And politicians are the ultimate debtors. But it kills the people in the middle class who have their savings denominated in dollars.

Being a responsible American worker, John Smith worked hard for 30 years to save a million dollars for retirement. Now that he's here, he finds that $1,000,000 is barely enough to sustain his family for 4 years, and it certainly will not last for the 20 years that they will live beyond retirement. John's son is paid $65,000 per year, which is more than the average worker. His pay raises of 2% per year are nothing compared to the real inflation, which is 15%. He now finds that his salary is not enough for him to live, so he's forced to find a second job or take out a loan.

What about the wealthy?
Those with lots of money are well-connected to politicians, or at least well-informed about true money. So, they do not hold onto dollars, because they know that FRNs are perpetually losing value. They make sure that their net worth is spread across various asset classes that are not affected by (or benefit from) inflation, such as real estate, stocks, ETFs, businesses, gold, silver, and most recently, cryptocurrencies.

What about the poor?
The poorest people don't have large amounts of savings, so the devaluation of the dollar does not hurt them much. In fact, the more debt they have, the better. If Joe Poor took out a $35,000 loan 20 years ago thinking it was a lot of money (it was), he worries about it *less* each day. In a few years, $35,000 will be peanuts. Also, the worse inflation gets, the more likely the poor may be to receive welfare from politicians. Additionally, welfare programs are generally indexed for inflation, meaning that the amount paid out to recipients increases as inflation devalues the dollar.

Chapter 2: The False Morality of Extortion

"I don't mind paying taxes! Politicians spend public funds on things that we all need, like roads, bridges, emergency services, and the military! You crazy anarchists are reckless and so unrealistic! Do you want to live with no fire department in your town and no military protecting our lives and our freedom?!"

We have all surely heard such statements before. Not only have I heard this statement thousands of times, but I was the one saying it on many occasions before I was freed from the mental shackles of statism (blind obedience to the state). Like nearly every other person on Earth, my parents and teachers taught me that paying taxes was the moral thing to do. I believed all the typical propaganda about how we all have moral obligations to society, how we are one collective group, and how the government takes a small amount of taxes from many people to maximize efficiency and provide everyone with the many great services that keep our society functioning so well.[34]

We will address some of the wasteful and malicious items that the government spends our tax dollars on in chapter seven.

Of course, only a small amount of tax money is used to fund truly necessary things like infrastructure and emergency services.

However, how would I feel about taxation if we lived in a world in which the government only spent our tax dollars on *necessary* things, such as roads, defense, and other absolutely critical programs? Would I support taxation if it contributed to no waste, fraud,[35] corruption, or terrorist funding?

I would still oppose those expenditures. Because they would still be funded by extortion.

In response to the common refrain that *"Taxes are the price we pay to live in civilized society,"* Spike Cohen, a libertarian activist, published the following statement:

"Taxes are the price we pay to not be arrested and have our assets and property seized . . . there are many ways to describe that arrangement, but 'civilized society' isn't one of them."

Once a person steals my money by force, it really does not matter much to me whether they use that stolen money to buy heroin for themselves or ice cream for orphans. The theft was immoral, so I do not support it.

"Alu, are you against ice cream for poor orphans???"

No. I am against theft. Don't hijack the subject by inappropriately focusing on the particular use of the stolen money.

If you stole $500 from your neighbor and then mowed his lawn, would he be happy, angry, or indifferent?

Of course, he would likely be extremely angry, because you stole money from him and provided a service that he did not request.

He also may not have wanted to give you the money, may not have wanted his lawn mowed, and may have felt that he could have gotten a better deal elsewhere.

While some people believe that we all consent to taxation on some level or in some ways, they cannot reconcile the extortion with those who unequivocally state that they *"DO NOT WISH TO PAY ANY TAXES AND WOULD LIKE TO OPT OUT OF ALL GOVERNMENT SERVICES."*

Whether we should support taxation comes down to one simple question: Is consent necessary, or is extortion acceptable?

Is it moral to pay taxes?
Now that we've established that the government obtains money from extortion[36] and uses that money for so many immoral purposes, we could surmise that paying taxes is not a moral act.

We must acknowledge that our tax dollars are used by evil politicians to abuse, control, and extort peaceful citizens in order to serve their own immoral and selfish interests. Often, tax dollars find their way to the most wicked people[37] in the world, including Xi Jinping, Vladimir Putin, terrorist regimes in Iran, Pakistan, Libya, Egypt, Hamas, and many others. Books such as *Secret Empires* by Peter Schweizer explain in great detail and with unimpeachable sources that politicians in the D.C. Empire have used our tax dollars to enrich themselves and their friends, who happen to be the most vicious dictators and oligarchs on Earth.

A common justification for taxation by religious statists is that the Bible (the New Testament, specifically) seems to support obeying the government and paying taxes. Romans 13 does say things like:

"For because of this you also pay taxes, for the authorities are ministers of God, attending to this very thing. Pay to all what is owed to them: taxes to whom taxes are owed, revenue to whom revenue is owed, respect to whom respect is owed, honor to whom honor is owed."

"Let every person be subject to the governing authorities. For there is no authority except from God, and those that exist have been instituted by God. Therefore whoever resists the authorities resists what God has appointed, and those who resist will incur judgment. For rulers are not a terror to good conduct, but to bad. Would you have no fear of the one who is in authority? Then do what is good, and you will receive his approval, for he is God's servant for your good. But if you do wrong, be afraid, for he does not bear the sword in vain. For he is

the servant of God, an avenger who carries out God's wrath on the wrongdoer. Therefore one must be in subjection, not only to avoid God's wrath but also for the sake of conscience."

"Therefore whoever resists the authorities resists what God has appointed, and those who resist will incur judgment."

To those who truly believe that we should obey the Bible to a tee, we could find plenty of support for freedom and plenty of reasons to abolish our current federal government if we are to obey the word of God. The original Bible – the Old Testament – makes it very clear that theft is wrong and that killing a thief is perfectly acceptable if one fears for one's life. Exodus 22 says:

"When a man steals an ox or a sheep and butchers it or sells it, he must repay five cattle for the ox or four sheep for the sheep. If a thief is caught in the act of breaking in, and he is beaten to death, no one is guilty of bloodshed."

Of course, if we were to suddenly begin to obey the word of God, we would have to put many people to death, as per the Bible:

"If there is a man who lies with a male as those who lie with a woman, both of them have committed a detestable act; they shall surely be put to death. Their bloodguiltiness is upon them."
- Leviticus 20

"Six days shall work be done, but on the seventh day there shall be to you a holy day, a sabbath of rest to the Lord: whosoever doeth work therein shall be put to death." - Exodus 35

"If there is a man who commits adultery with another man's wife, one who commits adultery with his friend's wife, the adulterer and the adulteress shall surely be put to death." – Leviticus 20

"If a man is found lying with a married woman, then both of them shall die, the man who lay with the woman, and the woman; thus you shall purge the evil from Israel." – Deuteronomy 22

"But that prophet or that dreamer of dreams shall be put to death, because he has taught rebellion against the Lord your God, who brought you out of the land of Egypt and redeemed you out of the house of slavery, to make you leave the way in which the Lord your God commanded you to walk. So you shall purge the evil from your midst." – Deuteronomy 13

"Anyone who curses their father or mother is to be put to death. Because they have cursed their father or mother, their blood will be on their own head." – Leviticus 20

"He that sacrificeth unto any god, save unto the Lord only, he shall be utterly destroyed." – Exodus 20

So, if the Bible were obeyed, many people and nearly every politician would no longer be alive, if you know what I mean.

Children are taught that it is moral to pay taxes and that our taxes help society become healthy and prosperous. In reality, our taxes fund dishonest politicians like the Bidens, Clintons, and Bushes. Our taxes fund ISIS.[38] Our taxes fund the DEA–the drug war agency. Our taxes are used to bribe states into abusing their own citizens. If you've paid taxes, you may not be an evil person, but you have given money to evil people and you have contributed to evil causes. While it seems like politicians have infinite power, they are nothing without their perpetual cash flow. And we can turn that flow off once we decide that we will refuse to be victims of theft.

Chapter 3: Taxation is Impractical

Setting aside the immorality of extortion, let's take a look at whether taxation is generally a net benefit, net detriment, or irrelevant to the economy and society at large.

Before we discuss the economy, it is important to understand what it is and how it works. In a society that is not manipulated by politicians, nearly every person would contribute something of value. They would offer goods or services to others in the society in exchange for money. In the absence of politicians to steal and redistribute wealth, each person would have to earn a living if they did not wish to starve to death. The most reliable way to earn money is to work. More specifically, the worker must produce value in order to earn money. Of course, a person might work very hard throwing bales of hay back and forth on his farm without earning any money. Thus, value production is not necessarily equivalent to effort.

People can only earn money when they make someone want to give them money. The only ways to make someone want to give you money are by offering them a product or service that they find valuable, by asking them for a charitable gift, or by threatening to harm them. Peaceful workers generally earn money via the first method; they earn it by way of consensual trade. Governments and their employees generally obtain money by using the third method; they threaten to use violence (arrest, prison, death) against those who do not pay regular extortion fees to their rulers.

Imagine that you owned a business that operated 1,500 fitness centers spread throughout the united states. Let's imagine that your annual revenue was $27 million and your annual expenses (including taxes) amounted to $24 million. On a simple level, this would leave you with a $3 million profit each year. That profit could be used to pay yourself and to reinvest into your company by expanding or improving the gyms. You may choose to pay yourself $1 million each year and reinvest the other two million into your business.

You always paid a 35% tax on the gross revenue of your business, but that rate was lowered to 21% when President Trump signed the Tax Cuts & Jobs Act into law in 2017. Still, you must pay the D.C. Empire $5,670,000 each year right off the bat, just to stay out of prison. You must also pay payroll taxes, property taxes, and many other taxes. You must also deal with the cost of federal regulations. This means that you must pay dozens of lawyers and compliance officers to ensure that you are not violating any of the millions of laws. If you don't comply perfectly with the sociopaths in suits, you may be kidnapped by men with guns. You wouldn't be the first gym owner to be punished for non-compliance[39] with the government gang. Worst of all, inflation caused by the federal reserve and the D.C. Empire's fiscal policy erodes your savings by the day.

Your employees each earn between $40,000 and $130,000 each year. You employ a total of 17,000 employees, including personal trainers, janitors, and gym managers. They each must give the government money again whenever they receive a paycheck. Each week, your average employee is extorted by politicians, who steal around 25% of their income. Of course, their income is taxed again whenever they buy items, invest, or do anything else that the government can find out about.

Now, imagine that the corporate tax was increased to 45% and the federal income tax brackets were each increased a few percentage points, as well. The government would surely frame the tax increase as a generous and benevolent act; for it would allow our gracious leaders in D.C. to give more money to poor and sick people. What effect would this 'generous' policy have on your business and your employees and clients?

As your annual business tax increases to around $10,000,000, you have to either increase your revenue, decrease your expenses, or close the business. The only possible options would be to decrease wages for your workers (the same workers who just lost money due to an increase in their income taxes), increase the costs for your customers, stop paying taxes and tell the government to stop extorting you or sell the business altogether. Are you beginning to see how increases in taxes hurt the economy?

As employees see their net earnings decrease, they become less incentivized to work. Often, increased taxes generally correspond with increased welfare (government-controlled redistribution of wealth). Once a given employee discovers that they are working their tail off for a net income of $27,000 per year because of extortion and that they could net $30,000 (or more) a year if they had no job and received welfare, their choice becomes obvious; they quit and go on welfare forever. Financially speaking, going on welfare is very often the wiser choice. Why work at a real job when you could make more money by sitting at home?

In total, there are around 100 different welfare programs administered by politicians. If a person is approved for a few of them, they could net up to $100,000 each year in benefits, including housing, medical insurance, food stamps, cash assistance, and more. Keep in mind that these benefits are not taxed, meaning that the net value of the benefits is the same as their gross value. Why work full time, earn modest money, give the government a quarter of it, and then use the rest for housing, food, and utilities, when you could just quit working and wait for government programs to pay for all of those things and more?

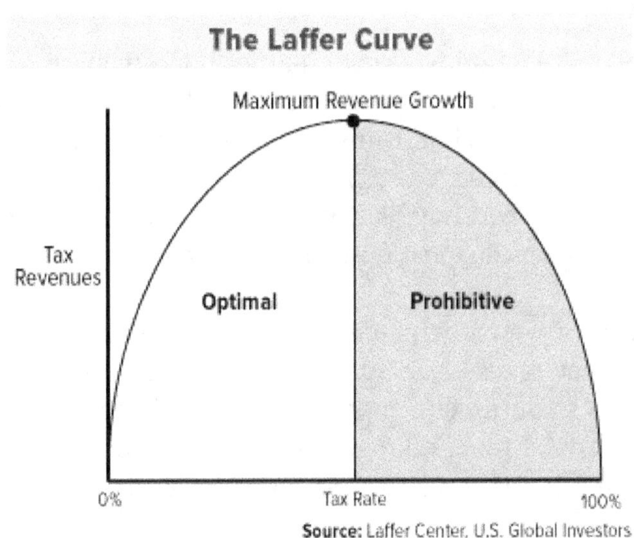

Source: Laffer Center, U.S. Global Investors

Furthermore, overall government revenues (how much the government collects via taxation) *decrease* as tax rates *increase.* Contrary to what you might have thought, increasing taxes does not necessarily correlate with more money for the government. As taxes are increased, workers tend to work less and collect welfare more, both of which strain the government instead of supporting it. Additionally, high earners grow more likely to hide, offshore, and manipulate their accounts in such a way that decreases their tax burden. The higher the tax rate, the more incentive billionaires and millionaires have to hide their money. If I stood to lose $17 million each year, I would certainly spend a few million dollars hiding money in Switzerland or the Caribbean. If my total tax burden was very low, I probably would not bother moving my accounts out of the united states.

In 1974, economist Art Laffer demonstrated this phenomenon to members of President Gerald Ford's administration. What came to be known as the 'Laffer Curve'[40] illustrated exactly how the government should choose a tax rate that is not too high[41] or too low if they hope to collect the most possible tax revenue.

This was proven when federal tax revenue increased[42] after Reagan cut taxes in 1980. Still, President Biden and the Democrats continue to support a massive increase in nearly every form of taxation. Some Marxists in the D.C. Empire are pushing for a new annual tax on each person's net worth.[43]

The bottom line is that taxation deters production. The higher the overall taxation, the fewer people will want to work, because the less value they would be able to keep for themselves.

I cannot say strongly enough that I 100% reject and condemn all theft, including taxation, even if it is minimal. Theft is immoral, regardless of the amount, the justification, or the result. However, if you do not care for morality, perhaps the impracticality of taxation can convince you to stop supporting the barbaric practice.

Without taxation, how could the government operate, though? Where would the money come from? Would the government cease to operate if it could not tax its serfs?

Chapter 4: Current State of The Theft

While some may think that eliminating taxation is a radical idea, consider that slavery and patriarchy were considered normal in almost every country throughout almost all of human history, whereas taxation (especially on income and sales) hardly existed in the united states until very recently.

It is common knowledge that the government is funded by taxation. On the federal level, the government collects around 3.5 trillion dollars per year via taxation and spends around 5 trillion dollars[44] per year. The gap between the two figures is currently around 1.5 trillion dollars and is called the 'budget deficit'. This generally causes the federal government to print more money and/or add to the national debt by borrowing from other countries or from the Federal Reserve.

The makers and the takers
Among the most well-known taxes in the united states is the federal income tax. The average American worker is forced by politicians to pay around 15-20% of their annual income to the federal government. Withholding – the practice in which employers hold onto a large portion of each employee's paycheck in order to give it to the government – makes this theft convenient for all parties involved. It also makes the largest tax almost unnoticeable to the victim of the theft.

As of this writing, the top marginal federal income tax bracket is 37%. The current brackets are 10%, 12%, 22%, 24%, 32%, 35%, and 37%. Each portion of income is taxed at the rate corresponding to its bracket. A common misconception is that those who earn more money pay more taxes because they pay the same percentage. However, the D.C. Empire punishes people for earning more money by stealing a higher *percentage* of their income progressively as they earn more! Therefore, the more one earns, the higher percentage of his income is confiscated by politicians. Because my gross income last year was in the 24% bracket, the various parts of my income were taxed at 10%, 12%, 22%, and 24%. After all of the mathematical calculations, my effective federal income tax rate last year was around 22.3%.

Tax Rate	Income Ranges (Single)	
10.00%	$0.00	$9,950.00
12.00%	$9,950.00	$40,525.00
22.00%	$40,525.00	$86,375.00
24.00%	$86,375.00	$164,925.00
32.00%	$164,925.00	$209,425.00
35.00%	$209,425.00	$523,600.00
37.00%	$523,600.00	

On top of the federal politicians stealing our income, state and city politicians often take their 'fair share' of what we rightfully earn. Some states take up to an additional 13% of the worker's income, and some cities take an additional 4%. So, if you work really hard, you may earn the privilege of the government and their thugs stealing around 50% of your income with only one type of tax. However, the income tax is just one of the many forms of taxes on our money, and keep in mind that politicians take another piece of your wealth at every stage of almost every transaction.

Who pays the taxes?

The latest government data shows that in 2018, the top 1% of income earners—those who earned more than $540,000—earned **21% of all income** but were forced to pay **40% of all federal income taxes**. This means that they paid an outsized portion of the federal taxes. The top 10% earned **48% of the income** and paid **71% of federal income taxes**. The bottom 50% of earners accounted for **12% of income** and **only 3% of taxes**. This means that in order to make the tax burden more fair, the government would need to raise taxes[45] on the poor and cut taxes[46] for the rich.

DO THE RICH PAY THEIR FAIR SHARE?

If you invested some of the money you were left with after the government stole a large chunk of it, you will be forced to pay taxes on any gains you have earned from your investments. Referred to by politicians as the capital gains tax, this extortion steals money from individuals who wish to increase their wealth by investing in businesses, property, or assets of any kind. The gains are generally considered part of one's income, so they will likely be taxed at around 20-30 percent, though long-term capital gains rates are generally lower. If you invest in funds or companies that pay dividends, you will be eligible to pay the dividend tax,[47] as well. No matter how you make money, including via the lottery[48] or bonuses,[49] (and even from gifts[50]) the greedy politicians will likely steal a large chunk of it. How wonderful!

More good news: Each April, unless your income and expenses are extremely simple, you will have to pay a professional at least a few hundred dollars to prepare and file your taxes, unless you want to risk paying more than your 'fair share' to the politicians. Without the professional tax preparer, you will not be able to sift through the 70,000 pages of federal tax codes[51] (not to mention state and local taxes), so you may overpay or end up in prison. The harder you work and the more sources of income you have, the more you will have to pay the professional who files your taxes.

The secret tax
Unless you are an employer, you have probably never heard of the 'payroll tax'. Whenever an employer pays an employee, the sociopaths who call themselves 'politicians'

get jealous of the money being given to the worker in exchange for their labor. So, they demand that the employer pay them some money each time they pay an employee. Currently, the federal payroll taxes[52] are social security, Medicare, unemployment insurance, and disability insurance, which total 9%. So, if you are an employer, you are forced by men with guns to give politicians $9 for every $100 you pay to your employees.

Sales taxes

Imagine that after the politicians stole a large portion of your money, you'd like to buy something nice for your wife. So, you buy a necklace for $200 from your local jeweler. Because your state politicians collect a sales tax, the jeweler charges you $227 for the necklace. Additionally, the politicians force the jeweler to give around 13.5% of his gross sales revenue (not his profit) to them, which also causes the price of the necklace to be inflated.

You also plan a nice little vacation for your family, including a resort with a tanning spa for your wife. You may soon have the pleasure of paying a massive tax on hotels (15% in Connecticut) and a special 10% federal sales tax on tanning,[53] thanks to a law signed by Obama in 2010.

Currently, all but five states levy an additional tax on the sales of goods and services. Here in New Hampshire, politicians often brag about not levying any general sales tax, but they do tax the sales of prepared meals, hotels, and rental cars. Many politicians in my wonderful state constantly try to expand the sales tax[54] to apply to more items.

Of course, any child could understand that punishing people by stealing their money each time they engage in consensual, mutually beneficial trade only discourages commerce or fuels black markets.

A federal sales tax seems inevitable, especially considering the trillions of dollars that politicians are planning to spend on universal healthcare, the Green New Deal, and much more. The Committee for a Responsible Federal Budget (CRFB) has calculated that a 42% federal sales[55] tax would be required if politicians hoped to pay for Medicare for all.

Property taxes
You worked extremely hard, pinched every penny, and stretched every dollar as far as it would go. Despite politicians (read: thieves) and their armed thugs stealing over half of your money already, you managed to pay off your house in 15 years, and you now own it outright. You have no more monthly bills other than utilities and food. Congratulations!

Not so fast.

Each month, you must still pay around $1,000 (far more in many locales) to government agents if you want to remain in your home. They call it a property tax, and if you don't pay it, the sociopaths will send men with guns to remove you from your home and kill you if you resist their efforts. Technically, people who must pay monthly in order to live in their house are called *renters*. However, renters generally agree to the terms of their lease. In the case of property taxes, the men with guns demanding your money make the arrangement seem much closer to 'extortion'.

Politicians claim that property taxes are primarily used to fund the community's government-run schools, but the same politicians do their best to make it impossible to get any of the money back if you don't use their schools. If your children are educated at home or in a private school (or if you have no children), you are still forced by men with guns to pay property taxes. If you are homosexual or sterile and cannot have children, you must still pay your monthly extortion fees to fund the government's indoctrination centers. No, you can never live rent-free in the united states, unless you live in one of the very few towns with no property tax.

Estate taxes
You have worked your whole life to build some wealth, and you have done a great job of it. You've paid millions of dollars to the D.C. Empire and to your state and city politicians. As you are nearing the end of your days, you speak with your children about the inheritance you plan to leave to them. Your daughter-in-law, who happens to be an accountant, informs you that they could be taxed at 40% by the federal government if you aren't very particular about how you transfer your estate to your heirs.

"What about the property?" you might ask.

"The thugs would steal 40% of the value of the property. So, unless we had the cash to pay that sum, we'd have to sell the house to afford the estate tax," she responds.

Asset forfeiture

Members of the organized crime syndicate known as "government" now steal more property each year than all non-governmental criminals combined. In 2014, government thugs used "asset forfeiture" to steal a whopping $4.5 billion,[56] which was more than the $3.9 billion stolen by common criminals during the same year. Over the past 20 years, cops have stolen $68 billion[57] from innocent individuals without any due process. Equally disturbing are the direct incentives for the theft. Most recently, a cop robbed a former D.C. Empire Marine at gunpoint for $87,000.[58] There was no reason, no conviction, and the cop did not even charge the victim with any crime. But under "civil asset forfeiture"[59] laws, cops can take any property at any time, as long as they "suspect" that it could be connected to a crime. What does that sound like to you? I call it "armed robbery." I addressed tyrannical asset forfeiture in greater detail in my book *Presumed Guilty*.[60] Most recently, FBI agents robbed[61] the safety deposit boxes of 800 people, stealing $86 million in cash, jewelry, and precious metals.

Ridiculous fees

In New Hampshire, we have no income tax and no general sales tax. While we do enjoy not having our income stolen by state politicians, we don't get off as easy as you might think. Our greedy politicians still confiscate thousands of dollars each year from us via property taxes and many small and large fees for things that should not be regulated at all.

One especially egregious example is the cost to register a vehicle in the "Live Free or Die" state. You might find yourself paying well over a thousand dollars to register your vehicle with the state government. Failure to do so will result in men with guns punishing you severely for driving without proper permission from the government. Politicians make matters worse by forcing us to pay them each year to fund the government workers who have the tremendously burdensome task of *not removing* our vehicles from their registry. The more valuable the vehicle, the higher your registration tax will be.

Despite paying many other taxes, we must pay additional fees to use the state parks, which the politicians and their armed men totally control. While in these parks, we must obey the politicians, and the parks are often closed to the public entirely.

All throughout the united states, you can expect to pay the politicians whenever you purchase a vehicle, register it, fill it with gas, park it, or drive it on a highway or bridge. All of these fees add up. Before moving to New Hampshire, I gave politicians over $3,000 a year at the tolls during my commute to and from work. And I never even drove on the Verrazano Bridge, whose $17 toll was the highest in NYC.

All Americans can expect to be taxed by politicians at literally every step throughout their day.

What a wonderful "land of the free" we live in!

In all, total taxation may account for around half of your income each year if you live in the united states. If 100% taxation is the definition of slavery (working for your masters and keeping no money for your labor), then does 50% total effective taxation make us half-slaves?

LIST OF TAXES

THE AVERAGE AMERICAN IS ASKED TO PAY

forced

Property Tax, Sales Tax, State Income Tax, Marriage License Fees, Local School Tax, Vehicle Registration Tax, Business Registration & Permit Fees, Waste Management Tax, Cigarette Tax, Court Fees, Dog License Tax, Drivers License Fees, Social Security Taxes, Gift Tax, Unemployment Taxes, Estate Tax, Fishing License Fees, Garbage Tax Gasoline Tax, Gun Ownership Fees, Highway Toll Fees, Hotel Tax, Hunting License Fees, Import Taxes, Individual Health Insurance Tax Inheritance Tax, Insect Control Tax, Inspection Fees, IRS Interest & Penalty Charges (tax on tax), Library Card Fees, License Plate Fees, Liquor Tax, Luxury Tax, Medicare Tax, Parking Meter Fees, Passport Fees, Air Transportation Tax, Biodiesel Fuel Tax, Professional License Fees, Recreational Vehicle Tax, Self-Employment Tax, Sewer & Water Tax, Service Charge Taxes, Sports Stadium Tax, State Park Entrance Fees, Tanning Tax, 911 Service Tax, Telephone Federal Excise & Universal Service Fees, Tire Tax, and most of all...

FEDERAL INCOME TAX

Chapter 5: The Hidden Tax

If we are to truly understand the full scope of the crime of taxation perpetrated by politicians, we must discuss the form of theft that is perhaps the most harmful—and the least visible.

In order to truly understand this form of robbery, it is critical to understand the purpose of currency. Many people live their entire lives without giving much thought to the definition or history of currency. Simply explained, currency developed naturally as a medium of exchange[62] in order to facilitate trade between individuals for products and services within a given economy. Currency could be thought of as a receipt that denotes services rendered or value that could be exchanged for a predetermined amount of product or services. Without these receipts, employers would have to pay their employees with physical products such as wheat or fish. This could make it difficult for the employee to trade their currency in the marketplace, because his products might spoil before he could trade all of them.

In order to be practical money, the currency[63] must never spoil, and it must be relatively scarce, relatively stable, and have clear indicators of quantity marked on each coin or note (1 ounce of silver, 1 ounce of gold, etc.) As you will learn throughout this book, the dollar is not stable, because it is rapidly declining in value by around 20% per year and around 99% over the past century.

Money simplifies and facilitates trade within a society. An excellent video[64] explains this concept quite well. Indeed, the last 15 seconds of the video are crucial to understanding this hidden tax that was created by a group of sinister politicians and bankers in 1910,[65] solidified by FDR in 1933, and augmented by Nixon in 1971.[66]

Before corrupt politicians and bankers created their joint venture in the 20th century, dollars in the united states represented real gold, which the federal government was obligated to grant the "bearer of the bill upon demand." In 1910, however, a group of the most powerful bankers and politicians held a secret meeting to discuss legislation about "banking regulation." The group included Nelson Aldrich (Republican Senator), A. Piatt Andrew (Assistant Secretary of the Treasury), Henry Davison (Senior Partner at JP Morgan), Frank Vanderlip (President of the National City Bank of New York, now Citibank), Benjamin Strong (Vice-President of Bankers Trust), and Paul Warburg (a board member of Wells Fargo & Company). At the meeting, the elites discussed and created[67] a banking cartel which would be partnered with and supported by the federal government. Three years after drawing up their plan, these authoritarians passed the Federal Reserve Act into law under the guise of 'banking regulation'. The Federal Reserve was a bank that could loan non-existent money to the federal government, which the federal government could then spend. Naturally, this caused massive inflation. The author of *The Creature From Jekyll Island* explains how inflation benefits politicians and big banks[68] and hurts Americans in speeches that could be found online (for now).

In 1933, Democratic hero, President Franklin D. Roosevelt criminalized the ownership of gold and demanded that all Americans hand over their gold to the Federal Reserve (whose board members are selected by the President, despite claims that the Fed is totally independent).

This began the authoritarian, tragic shift away from the gold standard that had backed the D.C. Empire's dollar since its inception. Now that the Federal Reserve—the joint venture between the government and the most powerful bankers of the era—owned nearly all of the gold in the united states, FDR could really put a dagger in the heart of American currency. In 1934, King Roosevelt declared that gold shall cost $35 per ounce.[69] This socialist, fascist president showed the American people the simplest example of authoritarian government-caused inflation. Yet, his sycophants continued to reelect him again and again. The D.C. politicians continued to empower the Federal Reserve and solidified their partnership with the banking cartel. In 1971, Republican President Richard Nixon officially moved the D.C. Empire's dollar off of the gold standard, putting the final nails in the coffin of our stable currency.

Even the united states government[70] readily admits that you would have to spend over $2,580 today to buy the same things that just $100 would buy in 1913. This translates to an inflation rate of over 2500% since the establishment of the Federal Reserve in 1913. If you open your wallet and look at

those paper bills, you'll notice that they say *Federal Reserve Note*. If you look at bills from before the creation of the Federal Reserve, that phrase does not exist. Instead, you might find phrases like *dollars*, *gold coin*, and *treasury note*, perhaps depending on the era. An increasing number of Americans are realizing that Federal Reserve notes have decreasing value with each passing day (current inflation is around 10% per year, according to the government. Many speculate that it's 20% or higher).

So, what should we do with our fiat currency which is perpetually plummeting in value?

1) Invest in commodities that are likely to hold their value: commodities with real uses are always a great option. Some examples of items that hold their value and/or have practical uses are tools, firearms, ammunition, imperishable food, water purifying systems, property, vehicles, computers, clothing, etc. Gold and silver have also retained their value since the dawn of time.

2) Invest in yourself: Your skills and experience could never be taken away by the government (unless they incarcerate or kill you—unlikely, though not entirely implausible). As long as you have the ability to build houses, treat the sick and the injured, write books, fix cars, or do anything else that people might value, you will likely be able to earn a living.

3) Consider using alternative currencies: An increasing number of people in the united states and around the world are transitioning to digital and physical currencies that are more likely to retain their value than the fake Federal Reserve notes currently issued by the D.C. Empire. Many people are excited about crypto-currencies because many of them have a finite amount of currency (technically making dilutionary inflation impossible) and because some of them are anonymous, unlike digital transactions involving Federal Reserve notes (digital transfers of dollars).

What is the motive?

Why do politicians love inflation so much?

The biggest reason for the elites' support of inflation is likely because it allows them to monetize the debt. Because our brilliant overlords' debt of 31 trillion dollars (and counting) is denominated in US dollars, that means that the less valuable each dollar becomes, the less burdensome their debt becomes. Again, to find the true value of something, we must compare it to stable indicators of value, such as one ounce of gold (which has pretty perfectly retained its real value forever), a month of living costs, or a month of wages.

If you owed a debt of $1,800 to a friend who required you to pay him back in a year, would you rather pay back that debt in the form of dollars (1,800) or gold (1 ounce)? Would you rather pay the debt now or in a year, when $1,800 will surely be worth much less in real value (it will buy fewer goods and services)?

In a year, an ounce of gold might be equivalent to around $2,000, so you'd choose to denominate your debt in dollars because dollars are rapidly losing value.

Similarly, the 30 trillion dollars that politicians owe will actually be worth less as time goes on. So, if politicians can steer inflation into the 10-15% per year zone or higher, their debt will soon be equivalent to much less actual value (by devaluing the dollar, they could theoretically pay off the debt with a few ounces of gold once each dollar becomes worth the same amount as Zimbabwe's money).

This concept is referred to as "monetizing the debt"[71] by economists, and it is no secret. Some Keynesian authoritarians do not see it as a very harmful practice, though. Once the dollar inevitably loses its status as the world reserve currency,[72] its value will really plummet, and it will die soon after that.

I have found a second major way that politicians benefit from inflation.

As inflation of the money supply causes the devaluation of each dollar, prices for all goods and services rise. Wages also rise along with everything else. Of course, the real effective value of the wages is not actually rising, because their monthly wage still only purchases the same amount of goods and services as their wages always have in the past. So, inflationary wage increases do not benefit workers, regardless of how much leftists and politicians might claim that it does.

For example, Sally earns $15,000 each year and pays $12,000 for all of her living expenses. Over the next few years, the 100% inflation causes everything to double in dollar amounts. Her living expenses have doubled to $24,000 each year. Her salary has doubled to $30,000 each year. Her disposable income has doubled from $3,000 to $6,000 per year, but it only buys the same amount of stuff as it always has. So, nothing has changed and she breaks even, right?

Not quite.

One major thing does change when wages increase: tax rates.

Rising wages don't just mean that the government takes more income because it's still taking the same *percentage* of your income. As people earn more money, the nasty politicians actually take a **higher percentage** of the money you earned. Sally's effective tax burden increased not just in dollars but in a real, meaningful way: *percentage*. Her real effective income tax rate went from **under 13% to over 20% because of inflation!**

Also, the savings that she has built up over the last 10 years has lost half of its value due to the brilliant politicians monetizing the debt. She saved up $35,000 over her career. Thanks to the D.C. Empire, that's barely worth anything now.

The kicker? Leftists like those at CNBC either fail to understand any of this or they actively neglect it when they publish headlines like this one:

The upside to inflation: rising wages

Jessica Dickler   6 hrs ago

- Although consumers may be paying more for everyday items, it's not all bad news.
- As inflation takes hold, wages may increase, too.

Bracket brilliance

For years, leftist socialists have been supporting massive increases in the minimum legal wage that a person could be paid. Currently, the federal minimum allowable wage is $7.25 per hour. However, progressive states have recently made it a crime for a person to work for less than $10 or

15^{73} per hour. The naive voters who were educated by government schools believe that increasing the minimum allowable wage helps them earn more money. They could not be more wrong, though.

To begin with, no wages should be dictated by anyone other than the two parties involved (the employer and the employee). Adults should have total freedom in trading their labor for wages, as long as it is a voluntary contract. Additionally, politicians should not be granted control over the most foundational part of our economy. In fact, the government has only one job: to protect the natural rights of people. And natural rights are life, liberty, and property. A high-paying job is not a right, and it certainly cannot be guaranteed by a politician without hurting others and largely distorting the economy.

First, when politicians make it a crime for a person to work for less than a certain amount (or a crime for an entrepreneur to pay less than a certain amount), there are consequences. When employees can no longer work for the

$9 per hour that the market has determined to be their value, they simply become unemployable. If you only produce $8 worth of value each hour, employers cannot afford to pay you $9/hour. It is simple arithmetic. So, the first consequence is a decrease in jobs for the lowest level of earners. If it cost you $100 to buy enough gasoline to get you to and from work, you would not work unless you made more than $100 each day. It's that simple.

Second, a consequence of forcefully increasing the wages for the lowest level of earners is wage inflation. If the lowest earners receive a raise doubling their wages, the level just above them will need a similar raise, otherwise they'd be earning substantially less than their subordinates. And then their supervisors would need a 200% pay increase. And so on, throughout the entire business and the whole economy. Doubling everyone's wages would cause a doubling in the payroll expense line of the operating expense for every business, which would cause them to increase the cost of their products and services for customers.

Third, as earners see their gross pay double, they move into much higher tax brackets overnight. For instance, a young fast food worker in NYC may pay an effective tax rate of *13% of his income*, which would be $1,900 of his annual $15,000 income.

Total income tax for $15,000/year

Your Income Taxes Breakdown

Tax Type	Marginal Tax Rate	Effective Tax Rate	2020 Taxes*
Federal	10.00%	1.73%	$260
FICA	7.65%	7.65%	$1,148
State	4.00%	1.87%	$280
Local	3.08%	1.44%	$215
Total Income Taxes		12.69%	$1,903
Income After Taxes			$13,097
Retirement Contributions			$0
Take-Home Pay			$13,097

But remember, politicians are greedy bastards by their nature. So, they use the brilliance of tax brackets and faux generosity to steal higher *percentages* from the people. Once the Democrats increased New York's minimum wage to $15/hour, increasing this worker's annual earnings to a minimum of $30,000, he was moved into much higher tax brackets. Now, the poor worker is robbed by politicians of $6,000 per year in income taxes, or *20% of his income*. Keep in mind that inflation means that each dollar becomes less valuable. However, once politicians can steal a fifth of the money from even the lowest earners instead of just a tenth of their money—while also appearing to be righteous saints for supporting a minimum wage increase—it's a slam dunk win for the politicians.

Total income tax for $30,000/year

Your Income Taxes Breakdown

Tax Type	Marginal Tax Rate	Effective Tax Rate	2020 Taxes*
Federal	12.00%	6.38%	$1,915
FICA	7.65%	7.65%	$2,295
State	6.09%	3.60%	$1,079
Local	3.76%	2.49%	$746
Total Income Taxes		20.11%	$6,034
Income After Taxes			$23,966
Retirement Contributions			$0
Take-Home Pay			$23,966

Of course, Corona–fascism brought about tremendous inflation due to the roughly 10 trillion dollars printed and spent by the federal government under the guise of "stimulating" the economy that they were actively destroying via lockdowns.[74] Throughout 2020, the federal government printed and spent unprecedented amounts of its fiat currency. The Federal Reserve, the central bank which controls the economy, played a massive part in Corona-inflation. The Fed brought the interest rate down to nearly zero, which caused people to remove money from their now-worthless savings accounts and instead buy commodities and assets, including in the stock market. This artificially boosted the stock market significantly. The low interest rates also meant that people were much more likely to take out loans, which also played a huge role in stimulating the economy. Remember, each loan by a bank (all of which are in the Federal Reserve/D.C. Empire banking system) creates new money, because the bank is authorized by the federal government to add the digital money to your account with a few simple clicks without physically moving gold or even dollar bills into your physical account. This expands the money supply. Therefore, every new loan expands the money supply, which is also referred to as "inflation." This leads to a devaluation of the dollar whenever the quantity of products does not rise at the same rate as the money supply. During corona-fascism, production in the united states actually *slowed drastically* due to politicians forcing nearly every business to shut down.

But the Fed did something else, which is extremely important, though nobody seemed to report on it at the time, possibly due to Corona-fascism overshadowing everything in early 2020.

On March 15th, FederalReserve.gov[75] (so much for the Fed being independent!) announced that they were totally abandoning the fractional reserve requirement for banks. The reserve requirement was 10% until that point, meaning that banks throughout the united states had to have at least 10% of the money they claimed to have on paper in their vaults at the end of each day. So, a bank with only 10 million dollars in its vault has been able to loan out a total of 100 million dollars, because they assumed that only 10% of depositors would ever want their money back at the same time. By my understanding, eliminating the reserve requirement meant that banks could now theoretically make infinite loans and claim to have infinite money on paper while having no actual money in their vaults. Even a child could see how problematic this could become.

Chapter 6: Tricks of the Tax Trade

Over the past few years, I've been combating government extortion as a writer, radio/podcast host, activist, and paid liberty advocate. During that time, I've learned some tricks used by tyrants to justify increasing taxes and creating new ones. This chapter will explore a few of the most depraved tricks that I have come across, as well as some of the most horrible expenditures made by politicians with our money.

Politicians are well aware that very few people in the united states truly want their taxes to increase. However, as control freaks and greedy bastards, increasing taxes is one of their favorite pastimes. So, they have discovered that whenever they wish to increase extortion or create entirely new forms of theft, they need to use certain language in the legislation in order to make it easy for constituents to digest.

In early 2018, as a relatively new liberty activist in New Hampshire, I learned this lesson firsthand. I was reviewing legislation when I came across House Bill 628. This bill's title indicated that it was about a "family and medical leave insurance program." The brilliant socialist sponsors of the bill used so many tried and true tactics in the language of HB628, and I called them out for each and every one in a 2018 article,[76] which I've reprinted below:

A great many residents of New Hampshire would tell you that their favorite thing about living in the Live Free or Die state is the absence of a state income tax. New Hampshire is one of only seven states that does not have an income tax. In addition to the thousands of dollars less per year that the

NH government forcibly takes from its citizens, the absence of a state income tax represents the NH culture—a culture of personal liberty and limited government.

However, some authoritarian politicians want that to end. The following 12 legislators have sponsored a bill that would effectively create and potentially impose a state income tax in NH:

SPONSORS: Rep. Gile, Merr. 27; Rep. Wallner, Merr. 10; Rep. LeBrun, Hills. 32; Rep. Rosenwald, Hills. 30; Rep. Fothergill, Coos 1; Rep. Gargasz, Hills. 27; Rep. McMahon, Rock. 7; Rep. Cilley, Straf. 4; Rep. King, Hills. 33; Sen. Woodburn, Dist 1; Sen. Fuller Clark, Dist 21; Sen. Feltes, Dist 15

How did they do it?

Authoritarian politicians can be quite manipulative. In crafting this bill, they used some of their tried and true tactics for passing anti-liberty legislation:

1) They are not calling it an income tax. The language of the bill softens the blow of a new income tax by referring to it as "insurance." They are well aware of how much heat they would take if they openly called for imposing an income tax on the residents of the most libertarian state in the union. Referring to the income tax as a "mandatory insurance fee that employers must withhold from each paycheck" makes it sound much less tyrannical than a new tax.

2) They are allowing people to opt out—at least for now. If you are familiar with government programs, you know how

easy it is to implement a "voluntary" system, which is then made mandatory before opponents can respond.

3) The tax is only 0.5% of each person's income—at least for now. If you are familiar with how taxes (especially income taxes) work, you know that they perpetually increase. (Refer to chapter 1: The History of Taxation.) This low figure softens the blow for the people who do not pay enough attention to comprehend what this bill really means.

4) In typical socialist fashion, they tug at the heartstrings of the productive individuals, because they know how compassionate we are. The bill mentions babies, adoptions, the sick, and the elderly. This makes HB628 extremely difficult to oppose without appearing heartless.

The bill summary: The bill establishes a paid family leave insurance program. It would be funded by a 0.5% income tax that employers would be required to withhold from all employees who do not opt out of the program. Then, when a person experienced a qualifying event, they would be paid 60% of their normal salary for up to 12 weeks. The state government would hold onto all the money in the fund. When asked why the people should entrust the government with even more of our money, House Commerce Committee Chairman Hunt dismissed the idea that the government handles money poorly and changed the subject.

Why can't these authoritarians just let people keep their money and choose whether to save, how much to save, and when to use their savings? Why can't they allow people to voluntarily buy insurance plans that cover these scenarios? Why must the government involve itself in everything?

The House Commerce Committee recommended the bill "Inexpedient to Legislate" which is generally good news, but does not bind the representatives to vote that way once the whole House votes on HB628. The Democrats on the committee voted "ought to pass with amendment."

In light of overwhelming testimony by government officials who calculated the potential numbers of the FMLI program created by HB628 demonstrating that the program would be gravely insolvent, Democrats on the committee proposed an amendment[77] that makes two large changes to the existing bill. House Democrats proposed to:

1) Cut the maximum amount of time a person could be paid for leave from 12 weeks to six weeks and

2) Increase the tax rate from 0.5% to 0.67%. I warned days prior to this hearing that this seemingly negligible tax rate would not remain so low forever. As it turns out, the rate has seemingly increased before HB628 even reached the Senate!

The House voted 186-164 to pass the bill with the above amendment. Unless Governor Sununu vetoes this bill (or some other miracle happens) New Hampshire residents should prepare to pay a 0.67% income tax. If you are an employer, prepare to withhold 0.67% of your employees' salaries and send it to the New Hampshire government.

After The Liberty Block published several articles, videos, and podcasts about HB628, reaching hundreds of thousands of readers and listeners, the bill failed in the Senate after passing the House.

Much of the confusion regarding HB628 revolved around the question of whether it proposed an income tax or a payroll tax. Ultimately, I asked the deputy commissioner of the Dept. of Employment Security (the government's expert who testified on the bill in the House) and he told me that it would technically create a payroll tax). So, I wrote an article[78] about the subtle—and sinister—differences between the two forms of theft of our earnings, which I have reprinted here:

In light of the recent contention regarding HB628 and whether it proposed the creation of a state income tax or an additional payroll tax, we felt that we should address the distinctions.

1) Payroll taxes seem benign to non-political workers, whereas "income tax" is a heinous term, especially in New Hampshire where there is technically no state income tax. Many people simply do not understand what a payroll tax is. Once people learn that employers are technically responsible for paying the tax, many of them assume that it's irrelevant to them. This benefits politicians who enjoy taking money from citizens in order to enrich themselves, their cronies, and to make themselves appear generous.

2) Payroll taxes are invisible to employees, whereas income taxes are plainly visible to every employee. Income taxes

appear on every paycheck, and the percentage and total dollars being taken by the government are clearly visible. Payroll taxes are rarely ever noticed by employees! Only the employer knows about this tax.

3) Government employees are immune to payroll taxes. The income tax draws from the income of all people who earn an income. This includes the ever-increasing demographic of government employees. We know that politicians often exempt themselves[79] from undesirable policies, but how could they exempt themselves from a new tax without looking like the elitist bastards they are? Enter: the payroll tax! Since the payroll tax technically places the burden on the employer to give the government cash every week based on the salary that he pays his employees, all government employees are automatically exempt. This is because their employer is the government, and it would therefore be theoretically impossible for their employer to owe a tax to the government! How clever!

4) A payroll tax has no real upper limit, whereas an income tax is limited to 100% of the worker's income (at which point the person would literally be a slave to the government). Since payroll taxes force the employer to pay the government, the government could take trillions of dollars a year from massive employers like Amazon, Walmart, Exxon, Apple, etc., and the majority of American employees might remain unaware of the tax increase, since their paychecks would not indicate that a higher percentage of their income has been withheld.

5) In order to ensure compliance with a payroll tax, politicians only need to force employers to comply. Technically, an income tax is much harder to enforce, because every individual must be controlled. If there are 100 million workers but only 8 million businesses, it would obviously be much easier to ensure compliance from every business than it would be to ensure that every individual worker complies with the tax.

The similarity: Both the income tax and the payroll tax are forms of theft and both are immoral.

Both decrease net income. Because payroll taxes make employers pay more money to employ workers and to run their business, the employer is left with less money after an increase in the payroll tax burden. This means that the employer is forced to cut spending either in the form of wage cuts, benefit cuts, or cuts in company investment (like new equipment, for example).

Keep these distinctions in mind the next time you hear a phrase like "*. . . funded by a payroll tax.*" Politicians will be shocked to hear their constituents call them out for proposing that massive entitlement programs be funded by payroll taxes. They think we are too foolish to understand how payroll taxes affect us.

Word games

For years, leftist tyrants (which describes nearly every person in DC) have used many deceptive techniques to advance their agenda. Their ultimate goal is to increase taxes, regulations, and control while empowering themselves and their cronies. The easiest way to accomplish this is not through brute force; tyrants prefer to convince people to vote for—or even to beg for—increases in taxes, regulations, prohibition, and governmental power. Often, this deception involves purposely conflating two similar terms,[80] between which most laypeople cannot distinguish.

On May 1st, 2021, Elizabeth Warren,[81] a communist senator representing the Marxist State of Massachusetts published the following statement:

"The bottom 99 percent paid 7.2% of their total wealth in taxes last year. But the top one-tenth of one percent—the top millionaires and billionaires—paid 3.2%. Less than half as much. That's not right. And that's one reason why it's time for a #WealthTax in America."

Rate	Taxable Income		
	Unmarried	Married	Heads of Households
10%	0–$9,700	0–$19,400	0-$13,850
12%	$9,701–$39,475	$19,401–$78,950	$13,851–$52,850
22%	$39,476–$84,200	$78,951–$168,400	$52,851–$84,200
24%	$84,201–$160,725	$168,401–$321,450	$84,201–$160,700
32%	$160,726–$204,100	$321,451–$408,200	$160,701–$204,100
35%	$204,101–$510,300	$408,201–$612,350	$204,001–$510,300
37%	$510,301 +	$612,351 +	$510,301+

Married filing separately pay at same rate as unmarried. Source: IRS

At first glance, nearly everyone misunderstands what the evil tyrant is saying. Naturally, when discussing the annual tax rates of rich people, nearly everyone assumes that the tax being discussed is the federal income tax. Currently, the federal income tax is divided into seven brackets, so that those who earn more pay more money—and a higher percentage of their annual income—than those who earn less. This is disgusting, unfair, and socialist, and it literally penalizes hard work and productivity. But it's not enough for sociopathic criminals who thrive on violating the natural rights of humans. Kleptomaniacs like Warren, Sanders, and nearly everyone else in D.C. want to create an entirely new tax to target the most productive people and the biggest job-creators in the union.

The tweet does not refer to the income tax. In addition to the income tax, the "Marxist Tax Act"[82] imposes a 2% tax on the net worth of wealthy people. So, if a person's total net worth is 10 times their annual income, they would essentially pay an extra 20% income tax. (So, their effective federal income tax burden might go from 30% to 50%.) Add all the other federal taxes, state taxes, and local taxes, and a person might have an effective total tax burden of 70%, which leftists would love.

Currently, the bill only seems to apply to those with a net worth of over $50 million, but amendments in the Senate or House could easily bring that number down to 10 million, one million, or less. Keep in mind that Biden spent his entire presidential campaign promising that nobody earning less than $400,000 per year would see a tax increase—and then he broke that promise[83] right after being sworn in.

Elizabeth Warren ✔ @ewarren · May 1
The bottom 99 percent paid 7.2% of their total wealth in taxes last year. But the top one-tenth of one percent—the top millionaires and billionaires—paid 3.2%. Less than half as much. That's not right. And that's one reason why it's time for a #WealthTax in America.

💬 735   ⟲ 6.8K   ♡ 30.4K   ⬆

Make no mistake; these evil communists believe that they are entitled to 100% of your property. They just believe that they "allow" you to keep some of your earnings each year. But they can end that generosity at any time.

Why should you care if the mega-wealthy people are taxed?

There are numerous reasons:

1. Taxation is theft, and theft is wrong, regardless of the amount, the reason, the perpetrator, or the victim.
2. As I mentioned, this tax could easily be expanded to also include people with your net worth.
3. All taxes roll downhill. If Bezos must pay billions of dollars per year in extra taxes, he must also increase the prices of his goods and services to compensate for the increase in taxes. (Remember my lessons about revenue and expenses?) If you don't want to see your Prime subscription—and all other goods and services you enjoy—increase by billions of dollars, you should not support a wealth tax, even on the richest people.
4. Inflation will also bridge the gap between the current threshold for the wealth tax and your net

worth. As the policy naturally expands to include more Americans, inflation will technically increase your total net worth. As the dollar loses value, your house, investments, and other assets will technically be worth more dollars. In 10 years, it's likely that 50 million Americans could be on the hook for paying this tax. By 2050, pretty much everyone will technically be a 'millionaire', thanks to inflation.

Double taxation

As you probably see by now, politicians are the greediest pieces of filth in this world. So greedy, they are, that they are not satisfied with extortion. The politicians in the federal government actually steal money from hard workers for the purported purpose of "helping them in retirement with social security," and then they tax the social security checks when they finally give the people their own money back. They literally tax the same money twice (not to mention the sales taxes, property taxes, and the other 90 taxes levied on the same one dollar).

Like most examples of socialism and fascism[84] that have occurred in our history, this tale begins with Democrat hero, FDR. President Roosevelt sold the idea as altruistic when he created the Social Security Administration[85]. In short, it's this great program that entails stealing income from people based on the false promise that they will get it back when the government decides that they are old enough to use it responsibly, which at the time was 65 years old. Later, this increased to 66 years old. And then 67. In a case of incredible irony, the government was proven to be the real irresponsible party when the public learned that they lost the money in the fund, causing social security to be insolvent. In a futile effort to save the program from going bankrupt, President Reagan and the Democrat House decided in 1984 that American seniors must pay income taxes on their social security checks. This is because those seniors likely paid many thousands of dollars into social security throughout their entire lives via taxation. This is a classic example of double taxation.

Grants
Each year, the federal government sends billions of extorted dollars to each state. Of course, this money was originally stolen from workers throughout the united states. When the D.C. politicians send the money back to each state, they place conditions on the state politicians in order to receive the funds. For instance, federal politicians could use extortion to bully a state into implementing common core, critical racist theory, sobriety checkpoints, gun control laws, and any other policy that proves difficult to implement legislatively. Even the NRA[86] has endorsed bills that give federal grants to states that implement increased gun control!

Behavior manipulation
It is well known that the government uses many different methods to control us and take our money. We often think about our overall tax burden (mine was 45% in 2016) and we notice some large increases in control, like the addition of 600 new speed cameras that technically violate NY state law.[87] A rarely considered tactic, however, is the use of fines and fees to deter or incentivize certain behaviors. There are certain things that city, state, and federal politicians don't

want people to do. But, in lieu of banning these things outright and risking public outrage, they raise money while guiding us subtly like the sheep that we evidently are.

Take parking meters, for example. They were first implemented in Oklahoma City in the 1930s to deter people from parking on certain streets. They were only upheld by the courts because they were used as a deterrent, and specifically *not* to generate revenue. Both reasons are certainly unethical, though. They have since been utilized in cities throughout the union. In 2011, the NYC government gang claimed 82,000 parking spaces[88] and demanded that anyone who parked there pay them money. Most of the spots would not allow drivers to park for more than an hour or two.

In 2012, they extorted over $200,000[89] from people by forcing them to pay before parking on their own roads. More importantly to the greedy gangsters, though, (who ironically consider conservatives the greedy ones) over $500,000,000 dollars was extorted from people in NYC who dared to park on their own roads that they already paid for with their taxes by issuing them parking tickets. That is more than half a billion dollars. But it's "not for revenue," according to the legal justification used by the government gang. If the NYC gang needed a certain amount of money for their annual budget, why not just apply that to income taxes? Why punish those who try to support the local economy by parking in front of small businesses?

Do Americans still know that all land is owned by the people and that the government was only created by the people to protect the natural rights of individuals?

It certainly seems like roads are owned by politicians, and not collectively by "the people." In socialist hellholes like NYC, if you were to ask somebody *"who owns the streets, trees, air, and the environment?"* nearly every individual would answer with some version of "the city," or "the government." And this is one of the most terrible things about the culture in socialist areas throughout the united states. The people are completely okay with being slaves to their government gang.

The same exact principle holds true with taxation for working and earning an income. Why work for a living if politicians on the city, state, and federal levels will all punish you for working, and steal a higher *percentage* of your money if you work harder in an effort to make more? And if you dare work over 40 hours in a week, you are essentially forced to give 50 percent more money to the government as an interest-free loan for the year. The income tax is also working well as a deterrent, as evidenced by the massive decrease in the workforce[90] since Obama took office. When Obama took office in 2008, 66 percent of adults in the union were working. As of 2017, only 62 percent of adults were working. Additionally, 16 million more people had to go on food stamps under Obama's destruction of the economy. Almost a sixth of the population is now receiving food stamps, taken directly from the paychecks of others.

Congratulations, socialists. You have successfully put in place a foundation that deters people from working. Soon enough, the majority of us will be on food stamps,[91] and we will run out of food and money just like Venezuela and many other communist countries throughout history. Unless one state can leave the union before it drowns.

"The problem with socialism is that you eventually run out of other people's money."

— Margaret Thatcher

Chapter 7: How Do Politicians Spend Taxes?

After stealing money from their serfs, the government generally spends the money in six different ways. Let's discuss each one.

1) Good expenditures
Politicians do occasionally spend the products of their theft to genuinely help people. While it may be difficult to prove that those who are helped by government programs would never have received the help from another source (or from their own effort), I would concede that a minuscule portion of government expenditures do provide a benefit for society or for some individuals. Local governments spend money on fire departments, many of which also provide emergency medical services to their town. While these services can and do function as volunteer or private organizations in other areas, this is technically a government expenditure that could help some people experiencing medical or fire–related emergencies. The federal government uses stolen money to help areas struck by natural disasters such as hurricanes, tornados, and floods. The D.C. Empire also spends billions subsidizing medical research, which could benefit some people. Many argue that subsidizing specific companies distorts the market because it puts the government's weight on the scales, favoring some companies over others. Far too often, the company benefiting from government policy has a connection to the elite decision makers in the government. Additionally, the more involved the federal government becomes in healthcare, the more control they have over health policy. And over the past few years, it seems like government officials are pushing disturbingly

racist policies in healthcare, de-prioritizing one race of people[92] in the medical treatment they receive. Still, there are a few rare instances in which government spending could benefit some people.

2) Neutral expenditures

The federal government spends millions on neutral endeavors such as 'the arts'. Other than the initial theft, this does not substantially harm or benefit people or society. That said, the D.C. Empire often supports racist museums and causes other controversies when they financially support the arts with tax dollars.

The Smithsonian Museum[93] is one example of federal tax dollars being used to promote racism and communism through "the arts." After years of somewhat subtle messaging condemning white people[94] and attacking the tradition of a nuclear family,[95] leftists have finally made their goals clear. They have officially stated in no uncertain terms that white people are inferior[96] to other races because they display certain characteristics. The government-funded Museum of Black Supremacy (officially named the "Smithsonian Museum of African American History & Culture") recently published an article on white privilege[97] which condemns all white people.

As with the last example, many also point out that art should be left to private individuals; it has survived since the dawn of time without being subsidized by politicians using stolen money, and it will continue to thrive without politicians supporting it with stolen money.

3) Bad expenditures

It is indisputable that the federal government spends a massive portion of the budget (possibly the majority) funding the endeavors that harm or abuse innocent citizens like you and me.

The federal government's largest expenditure is Social Security.[98] Nearly a trillion dollars is spent on Social Security benefits (paying back the money that politicians stole from people throughout their lives via taxation). When seniors finally get a tiny bit of their tax dollars back in the form of social security checks, politicians consider those checks to be "income." and they tax the serfs on those, too. At first glance, some might consider this program to be neutral. The government takes money from the serfs, stores it safely for them, and then returns the money to them when they retire. However, a deeper look illuminates the evil of this racket. First, politicians steal 12.4% of our money, which we could have used to buy a house, food, or to invest in our own future however we desired. The opportunity cost that they rob from us should be measured in the trillions. Second, instead of growing the massive retirement fund, the D.C. Empire managed the fund so terribly that it will be bankrupt by 2033.[99]

Politicians stole $1.4 billion from you in 2020 and used that money to pay armed men to punish you and your neighbors for owning firearms.[100]

Politicians stole $2.9 billion from you in 2020 and used that money to pay armed men to punish you and your neighbor for possessing drugs.[101]

Politicians stole $9 billion from you in 2020 and used that money to pay the 14,000 agents (some of which are also armed) to enforce enviro-fascism[102] on you and your neighbors.

All federal, state, and local police who enforce gun laws, corona-fascism, the drug war, illegal surveillance, unconstitutional sobriety checkpoints, and many other violations of natural rights are funded by your tax dollars. You are literally funding your own abuse.

It is now becoming clear that taxpayers[103] like you and I funded the corrupt Wuhan virology lab that created COVID. We were also forced to fund all of corona-fascism, including the very police departments that punished people for operating their businesses,[104] not wearing masks enough, or not receiving enough vaccines.[105]

The next largest expenditure is non-defense discretionary spending, totaling $639 billion. This includes federal programs related to education, housing, health, transportation, and other programs that the federal government has no business being involved in.

The D.C. politicians spend around $100 billion[106] on the Dept. of Education. This department exists primarily to brainwash children into supporting authoritarian government and opposing liberty. Government indoctrination centers are also increasingly used to convince children to change their gender,[107] to join the military,[108] or to make other life-altering decisions that their parents may find reprehensible. These schools focus less on teaching[109] useful knowledge and skills each year; their priority is preaching Marxism.

The federal politicians spend $623 billion annually on their military, most of which funds unnecessary perpetual wars, battles, and other illegal and immoral missions throughout nearly every State on Earth.[110] If you don't support policies that cause soldiers to get injured and die in battles totally unrelated to our interests and if you don't like that 20 veterans commit suicide every day,[111] you should stop paying for the D.C. Empire to do those things. If you want the military to station troops in less than 177 countries, you should stop funding the federal government!

The D.C. Empire spends $582 billion a year on Medicare—the money stolen from all workers throughout the union and given back to people over 65 in the form of a bureaucratic health insurance policy. Millions of workers are forced by the federal government to give thousands of dollars per year to D.C. politicians and bureaucrats so that politicians can claim to be righteous when they "give" Medicare benefits to the elderly.

Remember: every penny the government spends or gives must have first been taken from an American with the threat of force. Another way to look at this form of extortion is to imagine that if the entire Medicare system simply redistributed money from all workers to only the elderly[112] (which would still be immoral due to being theft, of course), each senior would receive roughly $11,000 cash per year, with which they could do whatever they desired. Instead, they are forced to rely on the government teat 24/7—and they have to vote, keeping in mind that politicians own them and could alter this system and change their healthcare coverage at any moment.

The federal government steals and spends $389 billion annually on Medicaid—a program that provides health insurance for people whose earnings are at or less than 133% of the poverty line.[113] Keep in mind that many people work off the books—or choose not to work despite being healthy—and still collect the welfare[114] benefits that you and I are forced to fund.

The federal government spends hundreds of billions of dollars a year on many other programs, many of which are inherently immoral, in addition to being funded by extortion. Many of those other expenditures fund other authoritarian, anti-freedom, statist agencies. The government spent $85 million building a hotel[115] in Afghanistan that could never be used. The government spends $4 billion annually on the FDA, which distorts[116] the free market and interferes with health care and medications. The FDA[117] is only one of around 400 federal agencies,[118] nearly all of which have the primary role of controlling your life and distorting the free market—and you pay for all of them!

American taxpayers essentially paid for brand new weapons for the Taliban, as well. When the Biden administration admitted defeat in Afghanistan and ceded the state to the Taliban, the D.C. Empire's military left behind billions of dollars worth of weapons[119] for the terrorists to use.

The federal government also uses the extorted money to control states, coercing state politicians to do their bidding. Nearly every state receives billions of dollars in federal 'grants' every year in exchange for using the money to implement policies that D.C. politicians desire. For instance, states have been bribed by federal grants to implement mandatory seat-belt laws.[120] Like many other states,[121] New Hampshire's police[122] have received federal grants for military vehicles[123] with which to terrorize citizens.[124] Police often operate warrantless checkpoints to "just make sure that every driver is sober" by stopping every vehicle and harassing and investigating every driver with federal grant money—because that's what the D.C. politicians want them to do. Where did the federal government get that money from? Well, you know the answer to that by now. They stole it from sheep from all over the union.

4) Waste
A massive portion of government spending could best be characterized as waste. Some of the most wasteful uses of taxpayer dollars included:

Teaching mountain lions to ride a treadmill:[125] $856,000

Studying[126] how many times "hangry" people stab a voodoo doll: $331,000

Studying the gambling habits of monkeys: $171,000

Synchronized swimming for sea monkeys: $307,524

Funding a global warming alarmist video game: $5.2 million

Developing a real-life Iron-Man suit: $80 million

Tweeting at terrorists: $3 million

Military equipment for Ukraine's government: Over $18 billion[127]

Dressing kids like fruits and vegetables: $5 million

Buying 24,000[128] Mine-Resistant, Ambush-Protected (MRAP) vehicles that needlessly killed[129] many of our soldiers: $50 billion

Studying whether Wikipedia is sexist: $202,000

Asking heavy drinkers not to drink via text message: $194,090

Government-funded ice cream: $1.2 million

A cup of coffee in the Air Force: over $1,200[130]

Since 1996, the D.C. Empire has spent over a **trillion** dollars[131] of your tax money to try to develop the ultimate fighter jet. The project is still a failure, and the plane still can't actually get off the ground.

The D.C. Empire's National Institutes of Health paid $387,000 to the National Center for Complementary and

Alternative Medicine in order to discern whether Swedish massages would be helpful for rabbits. There are likely millions of other examples of politicians wasting taxpayer dollars on ridiculous projects.

5) Foreign aid

Billions of dollars taken from taxpayers were sent to the hostile regime of Iran[132] by Obama in 2016. Of course, at least a large part of that money ended up in the hands of terrorists.[133] In 2020, the D.C. Empire passed a bill[134] that spent $900 billion on 'COVID relief'. Except that nearly all of the money was sent to foreign governments, many of which despise people like you and me. The bill sent 1.3 billion dollars of taxpayer money to Egypt for their military, and it sent millions to Cambodia, Sudan, Pakistan, and many other countries. It also spent tons of money on ridiculous items such as the reef in the Gulf Coast, creating a US–India Gandhi–King Development Foundation with an annual budget of $30,000,000, invasive species assessment, and much more. It also sent $10 million to Pakistan for gender studies, and the list[135] goes on. . . .

According to the federal government,[136] the politicians in D.C. send around $50 billion from you and me to politicians from 212 countries (pretty much every country on the planet). Those politicians generally pocket the money or use it to abuse their own citizens or to enrich American politicians. Very little foreign aid actually makes it to those in need.

The federal government also operates this incredible thing called the "export-import bank." The government program loans money to foreign companies. If the companies fail, the taxpayers bear the losses. If the companies succeed . . . eh, screw the taxpayers. Between 2007 and 2021, the program sent over $200 billion overseas,[137] only 27% of which went to small businesses (it mostly goes to companies like Boeing, Exxon, and General Election).

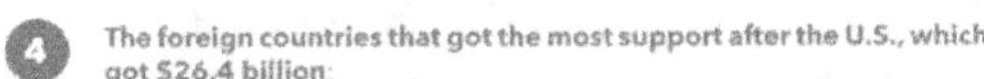

4. The foreign countries that got the most support after the U.S., which got $26.4 billion:

COUNTRY	AMOUNT (2007-2021)
MEXICO	$17,540,960,649.96
INDIA	$7,220,020,598.37
SAUDI ARABIA	$6,972,692,694.46
UNITED ARAB EMIRATES	$6,689,429,272.53
CHINA	$6,414,624,260.57
TURKEY	$6,248,758,353.95
IRELAND	$6,093,725,069.97
SOUTH KOREA	$5,177,585,744.09
AUSTRALIA	$5,101,452,191.84
BRAZIL	$4,082,362,302.33

3. The companies that got the most exporter benefits from the Bank are:

VENDOR	AMOUNT (2007-2021)
THE BOEING COMPANY	$66,434,545,437.09
BECHTEL CORPORATION	$5,045,305,225.70
GENERAL ELECTRIC INTERNATIONAL OPERATIONS COMPANY, INC.	$2,853,068,452.80
CBI AMERICAS LIMITED	$2,749,999,999.04
SOLAR TURBINES INCORPORATED	$2,716,112,540.54
EXXON MOBIL CORP.	$2,615,711,433.12
APPLIED MATERIALS INC.	$2,090,731,246.94
GENERAL ELECTRIC ENERGY PARTS, INC	$1,902,294,809.84
DIAMOND OFFSHORE DRILLING SERVICES	$1,900,000,000.00
BOEING SATELLITE SYSTEMS INTERNATIONAL, INC.	$1,485,316,457.68

6) Self-enrichment

It is common knowledge that politicians and other government officials use their power to make themselves and their friends wealthy. When you have trillions of dollars to play with, why not give billion-dollar contracts to your friends and relatives?

After initially lying and claiming that he didn't know anyone in the IRS, Braulio Castillo admitted that he was friends with an IRS contract officer, according to the Washington Examiner.[138] The House Investigation report found that: *"In 2012, Strong Castle won over a dozen contracts from the IRS with a potential value in excess of $500 million."* This was under the reign of President Obama.

In 2017, CBS[139] reported that Trump awarded a $300 million no-bid contract for Puerto Rico's recovery efforts to Whitefish Energy, a small company from Montana that had ties to Trump, his Energy Secretary, and his Interior Secretary. According to CBS: *"Whitefish is backed by HBC Investments. That firm's founder and general partner Joe Colonnetta gave $33,000 to the campaign of then-Texas Gov. Rick Perry, who is now Energy secretary. Colonnetta and his wife gave $28,200 to President Trump...Additionally, Whitefish founder and CEO Andy Techmanski knows Interior Secretary Ryan Zinke -- and Whitefish is based in Zinke's hometown."* After taking $300,000,000 from hard-working tax-paying fools like you and me, the company provided terrible energy service[140] to Puerto Rico.

Under Trump, over $13 billion in corona-fascism contracts went to corporations that heavily lobbied the Trump administration, according to CNBC.[141] In 2020, ProPublica[142] reported that *"Businesses tied to President Donald Trump's family and associates stand to receive as much as $21 million in government loans designed to shore up payroll expenses for companies struggling amid the coronavirus pandemic, according to federal data released Monday."*

President Biden and his family have already earned millions from their powerful roles in the government. After 50 years in D.C., Joe Biden is now worth millions. But his son Hunter seems to be the guy that receives most of the money on his behalf, including million-dollar sums from powerful players from Russia,[143] Ukraine,[144] China,[145] and others.

As reported by California Political Review:[146] *"A nonprofit that hired a Biden administration official received a huge no-bid government contract that wasted $17 million on unused hotel rooms for illegal immigrants, a federal audit[147] reveals. The politically connected group, which had no experience providing the services covered by the sole source federal contract, also failed to meet COVID-19 health[148] protocols required by the government when the deal was signed. The highly questionable arrangement was executed by Immigration and Customs Enforcement (ICE), the Homeland Security agency responsible for housing migrant families in detention."*

I am sure that every president and nearly every other government official engages in corruption. The temptation is too strong and the execution too easy. And even if they are caught, they almost never suffer any consequences, as we peasants would.

No wonder so many career politicians throughout the united states and throughout both major parties now have billions of dollars.[149]

Republicans who think that only Democrats are corrupt don't need to look very far if they wish to find corruption on their own side. From governor and congressman Greg Gianforte[150] to Mike Pence's chief of staff,[151] they are not hard to find. But my new favorite is Republican Senator Kelly Loeffler. She was appointed to the vacant Senate seat by Governor Brian Kemp, and she lost her election a year later. She and her husband are mega-wealthy. They also seem to be really good at picking the right stocks. She also knows just the right time to sell them—right before they crash! She sold between one and three million dollars[152] in stocks once she heard how badly the coronavirus was going to hurt the economy—but before the rest of the citizens heard the news. Being a U.S. Senator makes her privy to that sort of beneficial information. But she has a special advantage that even other swamp creatures could only dream about. She is married to the chairman of the New York Stock Exchange.

Plenty of Democratic politicians have made massive amounts of money through suspicious means, as well. Dianne Feinstein began her political career in 1970 and was the U.S. Senator from California from 1992 to 2021. Her husband is Richard Blum, and his investment firm manages $4.5 billion in assets. Democrats like Pritzker and Bloomberg are worth billions. Many books address corrupt American politicians, including multiple infuriating ones by Peter Schweizer and Dan Bongino.

Chapter 8: Taxation and Representation

Even children who attend government schools know by 2nd grade that the primary impetus for the American Revolution was taxation without representation. The famous story tells how King George and the British tyrants did not allow the colonists to have representation in the British parliament and that the state governors were appointed by the king and not elected by the people. Thus, the taxation was not predicated on laws truly representative of the people. So, the colonists rebelled and replaced the British government with a truly representative system; a just republic in which nobody's rights would ever be violated by the government.

This is a nice story, but so many important data points are missing.

From a 30 trillion foot view, there are two massive issues with this premise:

1) Individuals in the united states are hardly more represented in the government than the colonists were in the British parliament.

2) The overall effective tax rate for Americans in 2022 is orders of magnitude higher than the taxes paid by the colonists in the 1700s.

Yes, I will back up both of these claims. Right now.

We are NOT represented in the government, and I say this in all seriousness and with no partisan bitterness. We may have a negligible amount of representation in the federal government. We are also hardly represented in our state governments, and barely more represented in local governments. The American colonists did not get to vote for their rulers. But we barely have any influence over our rulers or our laws, either. To explain this and to provide evidence to support my claim, please consider the article[153] I wrote in 2018:

Any American who learned basic civics could tell you that the union is a representative republic and that its government is composed of three branches, as outlined by the U.S. Constitution. The Executive branch is comprised of the president, vice president, the cabinet, and a few executive agencies. The Judicial branch is comprised of the Supreme Court and the lower federal courts. The Legislative branch includes the House and the Senate. As you might remember learning in high school, the legislative branch writes the laws (legislation), the executive branch executes (enforces) the laws, and the judiciary branch clarifies the laws by making rulings on specific cases when there is a dispute regarding the meaning of the law.

We all learn that each of the 50 States is represented in the Senate by 2 Senators and in the House by a varying number of Representatives based on the population of the State. We are taught that legislation is written by and voted on by the House and the Senate and then signed into law (or vetoed) by the president. Thus, we all have representation in the legislative process in Washington D.C.

So, why do some Americans believe that they are not represented by D.C. politicians?

1) The Other Voters

In 2014, Jeanne Shaheen[154] received 251,184 votes from New Hampshire citizens, which amounted to 51.5% of the votes cast. This earned her a seat in the U.S. Senate. One could argue that she now represents the people who voted for her. But what about the 48.5% of New Hampshire voters who voted against her? And what about the additional 900,000 people in New Hampshire who did not vote at all? Basic arithmetic shows that fewer than 20% of the people in New Hampshire voted for Senator Shaheen. Yet, she won the election and became a high ruler for a six-year term!

It is difficult to make the argument that all 1.3 million Granite Staters' wishes are represented[155] by her in Washington DC. Those who support gun rights, low taxes, states' rights, and the right to life strongly oppose how she votes in the Senate. Some (arguably suffering from Stockholm Syndrome) might argue that Shaheen did receive over 50% of the votes cast, and therefore, she has the authority to represent every New Hampshire citizen, even when she supports authoritarian legislation that takes money[156] and liberty away from us all. I find this argument to be ridiculous, as even 99.9% of the vote could not give a person authority to steal what rightfully belongs to another person. Property rights are non-negotiable by anyone other than the property owner themselves.

However, many government officials are elected with much less than 50% of the vote. Carol Shea-Porter[157] was elected to the U.S. House to represent New Hampshire's 1st congressional district in 2016 with only 162,080 out of the 365,572 votes cast (44.3%). Thus, the pro-government advocate in this debate must concede that politicians who win elections could enjoy the moral authority to rule over others despite receiving less than half of the vote. And remember, only around a quarter of the people actually vote. In a state with one million people, all you need is the support of a few thousand people in the primary and around 100,000 people in the binary general election, and you become the ruler.

We don't even need to mention how party elites (Schumer, Pelosi, Clinton, McConnell, Ryan, Romney, etc.) often choose their party's nominees long before the actual primary occurs. Yes, primaries are generally rigged by party leaders. Both Republican and Democratic voters often have a horrible candidate shoved in their faces and are convinced to vote for their party's nominee because, *"He couldn't possibly be as bad as [insert opposing party's nominee]!"*

If you think that 44.3% of the vote might be too low to elect someone to power, guess how many New Jersey voters affirmatively supported Chris Christie in his 2013 gubernatorial primary. Given only a few choices, less than 4% of registered voters in NJ[158] expressed the opinion that Christie should be their governor. Those few votes did amount to the highest vote total among the Republican primary candidates. Christie went on to win the general election, largely because the Democratic nominee was even more hated by New Jersey's voters. Yet, every single human in the state had to obey his laws or face the wrath of his armed enforcers for four years. Over 96% of those registered to vote in New Jersey essentially voted *against* Christie. In a constitutional republic where natural rights were immune to legislative encroachments, such an election would not be a major blow to liberty. However, this union is shifting closer to a democratic oligarchy each year. Those who technically win elections[159] get to remove any rights and freedoms they wish. Nothing is off limits to our rulers. Not even our constitutional rights. After all, they were duly elected by the people!

If "Did Not Vote" Had Been A Candidate In The 2016 US Presidential Election

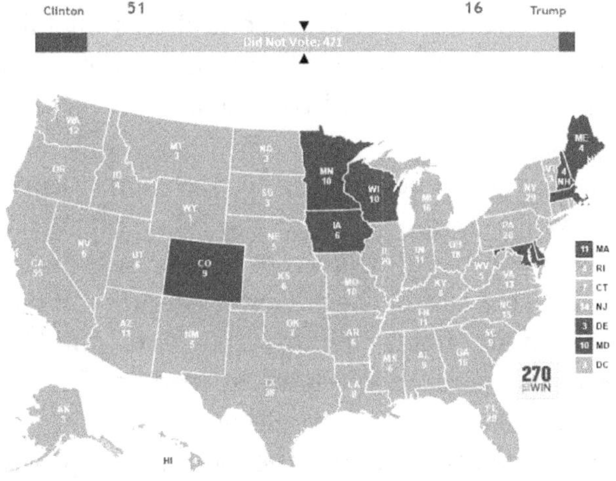

2) Who Writes Legislation?

Okay, imagine that we lived in a utopia where Senators and Representatives only won elections if they received 100% of the vote. In such a world, however, legislative procedure would remain the way it is today on Earth. Would I be satisfied?

Unfortunately, I would not be, because we still would not be represented in the legislative process. It turns out that not every Senator and Representative has the opportunity to author and propose bills. Well, I suppose that anyone could theoretically draft a bill, but leadership (the fine folks like Schumer, McConnell, Pelosi, Ryan, Obama, Clinton, Trump, Bush, etc.) retain roughly 100% control over which bills make it out of the committee and to the floor for a vote. If I were elected to the U.S. House with 100% of the vote from voters in my district, I still would have no real power. I could write and propose the most libertarian, constitutional bills, but it would be futile. Whichever committees my bills were assigned to would ensure (due to the commands from the leadership) that they were swiftly killed.

Additionally, the Republican and Democrat leaders in Congress write illegal[160] omnibus bills which contain thousands of pages and trillions of dollars in spending and then give it to the rest of the powerless Representatives and Senators[161] mere hours before the vote takes place. Legislators, therefore, don't have to read the bill. Even if they wanted to read it, they would not have nearly enough time. They already know that they will be supporting the bill—because that's what leadership demands.

3) The 4th Branch

As we discussed earlier, the U.S. Constitution created three branches of government. Nowhere in the Constitution are "agencies" granted the power to make laws.[162] Over a century ago, however, Congress and the President began to create agencies[163] in order to improve the "efficiency" of legislation. Unfortunately, Americans did not punish those congressmen, and the cancer[164] called "The 4th Branch" was born. Since its creation, the regulatory Goliath has grown to over 400 agencies, most of which have regulatory powers—that is, power to create laws,[165] and many of which have their own SWAT teams,[166] including AR-15s that you bought for the enforcers. Today, agencies[167] comprised of unelected, unaccountable bureaucrats create far more laws[168] than Congress does! Congressmen get to pass the buck and tell constituents that they can't be blamed for the new laws, the government gets to maintain and grow its control over our lives, and Americans like you and me get screwed. Perfect!

Did you really think that your Representatives and Senators would actually pass the laws that you elected them to pass?

4) Judicial Tyranny

Throughout the united states, on the federal, state, and local levels, courts usurp power from the citizenry, further diminishing their representation in the government. Considering that liberty and representative government are viewed by so many Americans as our union's greatest characteristics, this is troublesome.

The federal courts often block policies made by presidents and the Congress, essentially with no oversight or accountability. The Supreme Court regularly violates the (practically nonexistent) 9th and 10th amendments by ruling on cases that they have no business hearing—and then declaring their rulings to be "precedent" for all 340 million Americans indefinitely.

In 2012, the Supreme Court ruled that the Obamacare penalty was a tax, thereby saving the law from the GOP challenge: *"The Affordable Care Act's requirement that certain individuals pay a financial penalty for not obtaining health insurance may reasonably be characterized as a tax. Because the Constitution permits such a tax, it is not our role to forbid it, or to pass upon its wisdom or fairness."*

As Andrew McCarthy of the National Review explains: *"Yet, the narrow Court majority held that the mammoth statute could be upheld only as an exercise of Congress's power to tax — i.e., contrary to Obama's conscriptive theory, it was not within Congress's commerce power to coerce Americans, as a condition of living in this country, to purchase a commodity, including health insurance...We now know Obamacare was tax legislation. Consequently, it was undeniably a "bill for raising revenue," for which the Constitution mandates compliance with the Origination Clause (Art. I, Sec. 7). The Clause requires that tax bills must originate in the House of Representatives. Obamacare did not."*

Roberts stopped acting as a judge and effectively acted as a legislator when he rewrote Obamacare as a tax in order to save it from legitimate legal challenges. Obamacare marked the first time in history that Americans were punished for refusing to purchase a certain product, which in this case was health insurance.

Until recently, the Supreme Court had forced every state[169] (besides Nevada, which was grandfathered) to prohibit their citizens from betting on sports. The Court recently ruled that states and municipalities can force businesses located in other states to collect sales taxes on their behalf[170] when conducting online sales. President Trump applauded the ruling. If small businesses in New Hampshire obey this new federal law, they could go out of business. Were small business owners in New Hampshire represented in this judicial legislation?

State courts control whether state laws are legal and how congressional districts are drawn. Local judges are often powerful and corrupt,[171] as well. They regularly let other governmental criminals off of the hook. They regularly allow the city governments to steal land from innocent people. When a Connecticut town stole Suzette Kelo's house in order to give the land to a large business (Pfizer) that planned to move into town, the Connecticut Supreme Court justified the theft. On appeal, SCOTUS confirmed[172] that a city taking someone's home against their will in order to create economic development on the land does not violate the U.S. Constitution.

Books such as *Men In Black* and *XIV: How the Fourteenth Amendment Ate the First Ten* Discuss judicial tyranny in greater detail.

Felons
As soon as a person is convicted of a felony, they generally lose their right to vote for the rest of their lives. Yet, they are forced to pay taxes and obey all laws created by the

politicians despite having no say in who is elected to "represent" them. When the founders rebelled against Britain for the lack of representation in government and promised to allow all citizens to be represented in their new government, did they exclude felons[173] from being represented?

Minors

Individuals under the age of 18 can't vote in the united states. Toddlers three years of age can decide to get a sex change, but 17-year-old workers cannot vote. Yet, they must pay taxes on their earnings and obey all of the laws passed by their representatives. How is that not taxation without representation? Why are minors not exempt from paying taxes, at least? There is no logical way to argue that anyone should be forced to obey all laws and pay all taxes if they have zero representation in the government. Again, this exact grievance was the basis of the American Revolution.

Gerrymandering

State Representatives and Senators in each state are responsible for redrawing the borders of each congressional district every ten years. Naturally, both Republicans and Democrats work to secure some districts to be guaranteed wins for their parties. For example: If your state had 10 congressional seats, you would love to draw 4 districts that would be composed of voters who strongly support your party, making congressional wins easy every 2 years. Then, all you've had to do is win 2 more districts in your state and your party would own 6 out of the state's 10 districts. The opposing party's state and federal politicians would make deals with you that allow them to draw or gerrymander[174] 4 districts which give them easy victories. They're a confident bunch, so they believe that they can beat your party in the 2 competitive races in the state. Instead of districts being square or round, they are now often ridiculously contorted, long, complicated shapes.

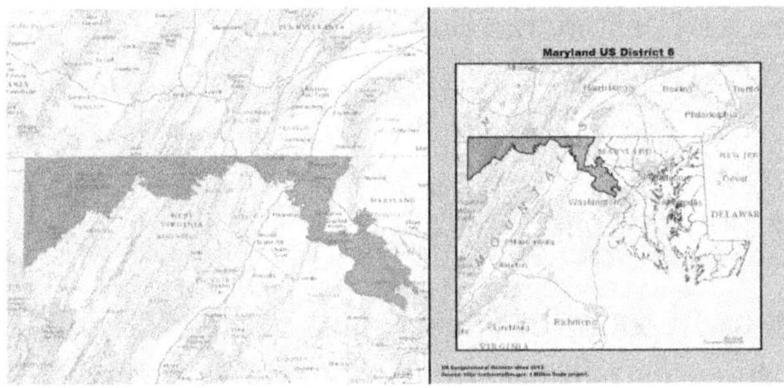

The more gerrymandered a district, the less meaningful each vote. Remember; politicians rigged the election by drawing the district in a way that includes far more of their supporters than the opposition's, rendering millions of votes meaningless. There is a famous saying: *"Voters should choose their politicians, politicians shouldn't be choosing their voters."*

Just as they do with "banking reform," every politician from both major parties claims to be the next Messiah by "ending gerrymandering once and for all" if elected. Yet, the issue is never fixed. And it never will be.

UN Resolutions
Of the 195 states on Earth, 193 of them are members of the United Nations. The UN can essentially create "laws" that apply to all 193 nations in the Union. The UN does have a

military, though they would be more likely to punish delinquent nations by using sanctions or other non-military punishments. Examples of recent UN "treaties" which made the news were the Paris Climate Accord[175] and the Arms Trade Treaty.[176] These laws affect you and me despite neither of us supporting the new 'treaties' and despite nobody in the UN representing people like you and me.

Lobbyists

One large issue that is hardly disputed on a partisan basis entails lobbyists. The short story is this: as long as we have a right to freedom of speech and expression, individuals and businesses will use their money, resources, and voices to influence legislation and policy. While this is preferable to the alternative (the restriction of free speech), the government will inevitably be affected by lobbyists who are paid by companies to speak out and/or bribe legislators. The more powerful the government, the more control lobbyists[177] have over the citizenry.

Voter fraud and hacking

There are likely millions of improper votes cast in the united states each election cycle. Many deceased people remain on voter rolls throughout the union, and many people vote more than once.[178] Additionally, electronic voting methods are much easier to hack than people would like to believe. A young child hacked Florida's voting system[179] in under 10 minutes, changing the outcome of an election. In 2020, Biden was elected with the help of overwhelming amounts of cheating,[180] more of which is coming to light each day. Every instance of fraud disenfranchises voters who believe that they are participating in a "representative democratic republic" by casting a ballot for their preferred leader.

Quid pro quo
It is standard practice for politicians to receive "donations" from their cronies and then award them tremendous government contracts (read: give them taxpayer money) in exchange for their donations. This is corruption,[181] plain and simple. Again, read Peter Schweizer's books for countless examples of terrifying corruption.

The only solution is to consistently seize power back from the government. Once the government becomes less powerful than the individual, all the unrepresentative issues highlighted by this chapter will hardly even seem to be a problem. After all, who cares how terrible a government is if the government is too weak to hurt you?

Even the Constitution gives politicians no authority
Lysander Spooner explained that the Constitution could not possibly grant authority to politicians over those who did not consent. Only a few people actually attended the constitutional convention and consented to the constitution. Only a few leaders of each state ratified the constitution. All those who opposed the constitution never consented to anything, and certainly did not give up their rights or outsource their liberties to any "government" official. Furthermore, as Spooner explains in his book *No Treason: The Constitution of No Authority*, it is ridiculous, tyrannical, and monarchistic to claim that all future descendants and immigrants should be bound by

agreements made hundreds of years prior. In contract law, we can only consent to render services or grant authority to others on our own behalf, and possibly on behalf of children as long as they are already born and are still minors, and only in very limited circumstances. We cannot sign contracts enslaving our great-grandchildren to any particular (or non-specific) group of people.

"But whether the Constitution really be one thing, or another, this much is certain - that it has either authorized such a government as we have had, or has been powerless to prevent it. In either case, it is unfit to exist." — Lysander Spooner

As for the second argument, that taxation now is much higher than it was when colonists rebelled against taxation:

We learned earlier that the total effective tax burden for hard-working Americans may be around 50%, making us half-slaves. Between the federal income taxes, state income taxes, city income taxes, sales taxes, property taxes, and the 90 other taxes, we are only left with around half of our money, despite rightfully earning 100% of it and consenting to give up 0% of it.

What were tax rates like under the British tyranny that led our forefathers to rebel?

The British hardly taxed the colonists. They had low taxes on imports (tariffs) and some poll taxes, as explained in chapter one. The property taxes[182] required by the British king were around "several shillings for each hundred acres of land." Each shilling was worth roughly half a day of wages circa 1700. The total tax burden for the colonists was 1 shilling per year, according to a study[183] published by the National Bureau of Economic Research. Of course, even stealing one penny for each $1,000 earned by a worker is still theft, and it is still immoral. The colonists' British counterparts paid 26 shillings per year, according to the study. Compare the minuscule tax rates of the British Empire to the massive taxes imposed on us by the D.C. Empire and its state and local politicians.

Regardless, many Americans insist that they will rebel against the government "when they become tyrannical." If tyranny is their trigger, what are they waiting for? A total effective tax burden of 50%? Total slavery?

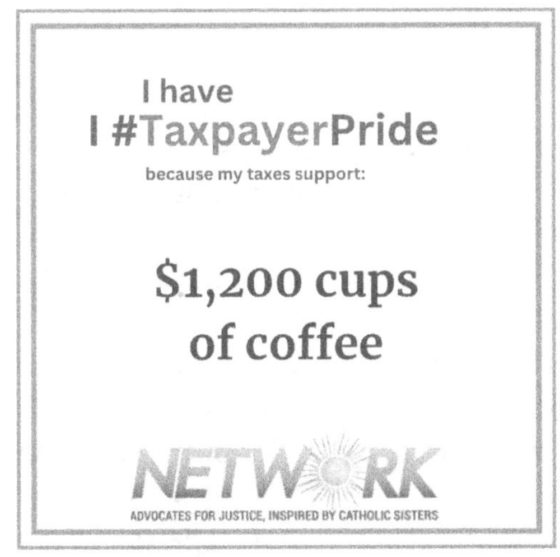

Chapter 9: The Welfare Conundrum

Let's be honest: do you currently receive any money from the government? Have you ever accepted any financial assistance from the government? Did you receive a "stimulus" from D.C. during the era of corona-fascism? Many taxpayers in the united states likely received at least a few hundred dollars from the federal government over the past two years. Many conservatives and libertarians who believe in little to no taxation—and who claim that they would never accept any money from the government—have taken money in the form of college aid, student loans, or the newly existent "COVID stimulus checks."

I have said for years that I have never taken welfare and that I would never want to accept any money from the government gang.

First, I believe that handouts are unbecoming for a respectable person who is able-bodied. Second, I believe that all the money that the government has is generally dirty money because it was taken by brute force, and I do not want to support theft. I have surely said many times on my talk radio show that I would never accept any welfare. Yet, I cashed the checks[184] that I received during corona-fascism. In fact, when Dictator Sununu made the strange decision to give emergency workers a weekly stipend[185] from the New Hampshire state government (despite those workers being the ones who were employed and doing fine while their "non-essential" counterparts lost their jobs and experienced actual financial hardship), I did not send the money back to the government; I happily accepted it. Does that make me a hypocrite? Should I have my "libertarian" card revoked?

True to human nature, I quickly rationalized my decision to accept the money from the government.

"Well . . . I have been paying around $25,000 per year to the federal government since I began working, which was over 10 years ago. So, until the government gives me back $250,000, I shouldn't feel too guilty about taking the money," I thought to myself.

Of course, if you apply a standard interest rate for the loans that I essentially gave to the government over the past 10 years, I could figure that it would owe me $300,000–$500,000 and possibly much more. The cost of government regulations on businesses in the united states is far more than $2 trillion[186] per year. Divide that figure by the number of workers (165 million), and one could deduce that the government owes each worker an extra $1,200 per year. Add all the pain and suffering that the government causes us, and . . . well, you get the point. I am unprincipled and I am doing mental gymnastics to try to justify my hypocrisy.

A few months ago, I was speaking with my wife about her elderly parents accepting Medicaid. Her parents are immigrants from the Philippines, and they recently completed the long and expensive citizenship process for the united states. Her mother is a cancer survivor, and her father has complicated metastatic cancer which has already taken his thyroid and his larynx and is now in his upper spinal cord. As you might imagine, his medical bills could easily become unmanageable. Is it moral for him to accept Medicaid, Medicare, food stamps, or other forms of welfare? Should I support his decision to accept government aid, or should I condemn all welfare like I've been doing for my entire adult life?

During the conversation with my wife, I was initially a little judgmental and unhappy about the prospect of my in-laws accepting government handouts. And then I began to think about my net financial transfers to the government throughout my life. I had paid hundreds of thousands of my hard-earned dollars to the federal government (granted, I only paid taxes under threat of force) and I've gotten nothing but tyranny and some interstate roads in return. If my in-laws could get some of that money back, I should be happy!

By the end of our conversation, I was more than fine with the idea of my wife's parents taking a tiny bit of money back from D.C. politicians. Furthermore, the less money D.C. politicians have, the fewer bombs they can drop on innocent people, and the less tyranny they could impose on citizens like you and me domestically. Every dollar kept out of the hands of the ATF, IRS, and other gangsters is a win for peace, prosperity, liberty, and humanity.

Remember, politicians can only do six things with the money they steal from us:

1) Things that help people
2) Things that are neutral
3) Things that harm people

4) Waste
5) Foreign aid
6) Self-enrichment

Of the six different ways that politicians spend our money, four of them are bad for us, one is neutral, and one is somewhat good, but rarely ever applicable. So, the more money we can keep out of politicians' hands, the better.

I know very few conservatives, libertarians, anarchists, and voluntaryists who never accept any money from the government. So, how could those same people condemn taxation and welfare? Are we all hypocrites with no principles?

One of the inadvertent outcomes of this phenomenon is that the acceptance of money from the government rattles libertarians by forcing them to doubt their own principles. I can't imagine that politicians did this on purpose, but if the greatest assets that libertarians have are their reliable principles, then attacking those principles and making them question their piety may be the ultimate tactic to destroy their movement.

My biggest takeaway from this issue is that the only solution to this messy dilemma—which is also the perfect solution—is to abolish taxation and welfare entirely. Then, we could retain our principles, our freedom, and our property. Once extortion is no longer tolerated, individuals could once again advocate for complete freedom and denounce all theft and welfare without (somewhat justifiably) being labeled as hypocrites.

Chapter 10: Modern Capitalism & The New Free Market

I'm currently learning German in the comfort of my own home without paying a dime for lessons. I'm also working on improving my Spanish, and I'm getting my childhood Hebrew back. I've used this same free education method to study medicine, chemistry, fitness, martial arts, music, and many other subjects. I am doing all of this without paying a penny in tuition—and without illegally using any programs or files. I am not stealing anything nor am I coercing or hurting a soul. Every single facet of my education is consensual and mutually beneficial to all parties involved. Not only am I attaining a free education, but every other party involved in teaching me is gaining something that they consider valuable, as well.

How could this possibly be?

Podcasts

I have only recently begun to utilize podcasts, and I find that they are extremely helpful. Unlike apps like YouTube, podcasts continue to play regardless of what my phone is doing, so I can throw it in my pocket and go about my day while learning. I subscribe to a few political, medical, and language-learning podcasts, but I've mostly been listening to the Spanish ones recently. Of course, they are all free. I receive value in the form of free educational content. The creators earn money via ads, promotions, affiliates, and live-reads. And the podcast hosting platforms earn money from the creators and/or from ads. Everyone is happy and nobody is violated. Podcasts are a great example of the beauty of spontaneous order[187] and what I refer to as the "new free market."

Website traffic

Nearly every one of the billions of websites on the internet has one primary objective: to get as many website visitors as possible. This objective accomplishes two important goals. First, the more visitors to the site, the more potential customers. People can't buy your products if they never see them. And many who visit your site "just to browse" may end up making a purchase. Second, the more visits a website has, the more money it can earn from advertisers. As you likely know already, the more eyes see your property, the more you could charge advertisers to purchase or rent that virtual billboard.

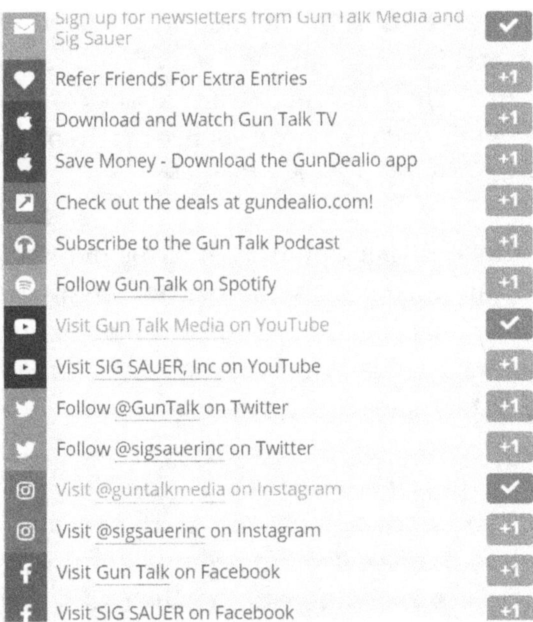

Considering the above economic infrastructure, businesses are willing to spend a fair amount of money in order to drive millions more visitors to their sites. So, they do just that: They team up with companies in adjacent industries and create large "giveaways" which feature prizes (free guns, holsters, ammo, gift cards, etc.) in exchange for people fulfilling a few tasks. For each task they accomplish, they receive one or multiple entries into the raffle. The tasks include entering your email address (a valuable piece of information for marketing) and then visiting each company's website and social media accounts. Some also reward users for subscribing to the companies' accounts on video platforms. Giveaways range from cheap holsters to $15,000 firearms.

As we always see with the free market, all parties benefit from a transaction that nobody is coerced into. The companies receive exposure via advertising and visits to their websites. The customers learn about companies they are interested in and they get a chance to win products they enjoy. Everyone wins and nobody loses.

I initially thought that only the firearms industry did this, and then I saw this exact same method being used by the Better Sax[188] YouTube Channel and saxophone company. That's when this brilliant form of the new free market—and its infinite potential—truly hit me.

YouTube

I use YouTube and other video platforms for language lessons and to practice listening comprehension by finding videos on topics that interest me, such as sports, music, medicine, politics, investing, guns, etc. I often watch videos from Khan Academy, Osmosis, Medcram, Ninja Nerd Science, Crash Course, Demolition Ranch, IraqVeteran8888, How to Spanish, and many others.

Over the past few years, free online education has exploded in popularity, primarily via video streaming platforms. One Indian man inadvertently created a leading free education platform when he was tutoring his cousin in mathematics in 2004. A hedge-fund manager by trade, Salman Khan recorded instructional math videos for his cousin to watch on her own time. He was very good at explaining things, so his videos became popular online. He continued making videos, and eventually brought on other expert instructors to make more videos. As of this writing, Khan Academy's YouTube channel has over 7 million subscribers[189] and has helped billions of people learn countless subjects for free. The site has since grown into quite a large online school, complete with personal profiles, classes, and many more free resources for students. Khan Academy is a non-profit which relies solely on philanthropy, and they seemingly do not utilize YouTube to run ads on their videos, which could earn them tremendous amounts of money. The school remains free to all learners.

There is an easier approach to free online education from the creator's perspective, though. Many YouTube channels do not want to rely on the generosity of others, so they rely on their greed and self-interest, which are the most fundamental of human traits. YouTube channels like MedCram[190] and Osmosis[191] offer people high quality medical education for free. The doctors who create these videos clearly pour thousands of hours of labor into their videos so you and I can learn for free. Why do they do it?

Greed, as I said, is the ultimate human incentive. Humans love money. We love value. We understand that time and resources are finite and that knowledge is valuable. So, we naturally desire to obtain as much valuable information and resources as possible while spending as little time and resources as possible. They may love medicine and they may love teaching and helping people, but money is what drives them—and allows them—to make these videos. Like you, I am greedy, so I don't want to spend $50,000 each year and travel to a college to learn what I can learn for free from my couch.

Here's how it works: the better their videos, the more people watch them. The more views they attain, the more money YouTube can make by showing ads to viewers before, during, and after their videos. The creators receive a large portion (around 50%, in some cases) of the money YouTube earns from the businesses paying for the advertisements. Everyone is happy, and nobody is violated. And you and I get incredible education for free!

Decent YouTubers can earn $20,000-$30,000 in a MONTH. Nate O'Brien[192] is just one example. He has over a million subscribers and gets a few million views on his videos about personal finance. He earns around a quarter of a million dollars per year from YouTube ads on his videos. The really popular YouTubers (and the attractive women) earn multiples of what Nate earns. Mr. Beast is a 23-year-old who earned $54 million[193] in 2021 from YouTube ads.

The New Free Market

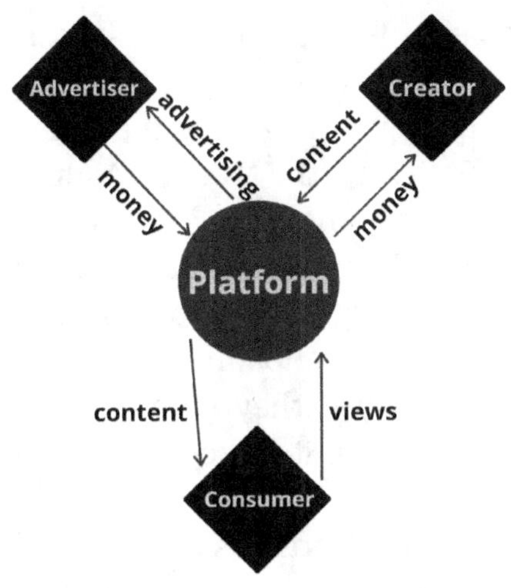

Other than surgery and a few other super-technical skills, you can learn damn near anything for free from the comfort of your own home by using technology (and books). If you enjoy videos, Duolingo, podcasts, or any other form of free education, you have spontaneous order and the free market to thank, not government officials or central planners.

This same model is utilized across many other industries, including government agencies. But it should be used much more. I believe that if we embrace the new free market and the incredible power and efficiency of advertising, we could fund governments without any taxation whatsoever. Technology and human advancement have demonstrated that anything, from videos[194] to billboards,[195] to buses & trains,[196] and even buildings[197] and roads,[198] can earn money for their owner. As long as people see it, it could be leased to businesses who are willing to pay billions[199] to advertise their products on highly visible properties or online spaces.

If they were able to, I'm sure that businesses would pay a few dollars to place their ads or logos on municipal roads, vehicles, and buildings. Imagine if the federal government streamed the State of the Union Address (and every congressional hearing and vote) on YouTube or a similar platform. They would get hundreds of millions of views. This could translate to billions of dollars a year, which would eventually be enough to fund the federal government, especially if they trimmed some fat[200] from their budget. If we took it a step further, we could lease every square inch of all 640 million acres of federal land[201] to the highest paying advertisers to fund the federal budget. If we truly utilized the power of advertising to its full potential, it might bring in so much money that the federal government would have a surplus. The D.C. politicians could then use this extra money for welfare, to pay down the national debt, or to reimburse people like you and me for years of extortion and abuse.

Think about it: Federal politicians already sell their souls[202] to rich corporate interests (not to mention foreign governments[203]) by way of lobbying, donations, and simple bribes. They are benefiting from big companies spending billions of dollars. Why shouldn't "we the people" benefit a bit from the companies' expenditures, too? Instead of spending millions on buying politicians, maybe Boeing would pay a few million dollars to have their logo placed on a wall in the U.S. Senate for a week. I would rather see a

Boeing logo on the Senate wall on C-Span than be extorted for $20,000 by Biden and Pelosi each year. Which would you prefer? Being taxed into bankruptcy or occasionally seeing some ads?

Considering how modern anti-freedom activists[204] and authoritarian politicians[205] claim that free market capitalism is outdated, the truth is that they have it backwards. The free market and spontaneous order could never be obsolete because they are the essence of a free world, progress, and prosperity. Central planners like politicians, regulators, and judges never could have invented products or created economic models such as the one described above; these things must develop naturally based on human greed—the same trait that politicians[206] ironically promise to eliminate from society for good.

Lottery
Like every other state in the union, the New Hampshire government operates a lottery system. Many stores throughout the state sell the lottery[207] tickets. A quarter of the gross proceeds go to the state government's budget for education. This program has contributed nearly $2 billion to the state's education budget since its inception in 1964. Unlike taxation, which is collected using the threat of violence or prison, people purchase lottery tickets of their own volition—whenever they feel like it!

If the government operates more lotteries, improves its efficiency, or spends less money each year, this revenue stream could fund a large portion of the state government's annual budget. This method of revenue generation cannot be denied. It is literally already being utilized.

Fee for service

While I hesitate to endorse any government entity, especially those that allow politicians to involve themselves in the economy, some services do provide another tool that the government could utilize to generate revenue without the use of force. The federal government courier service currently brings in $77 billion[208] per year delivering mail and packages. The Postal Service's revenue nearly pays for the whole agency, which is impressive for a government-run endeavor. The New Hampshire government currently operates 82 liquor stores. The prices and products are attractive, they are tax-free, and the selection is large, so consumers voluntarily give their money to the government stores in exchange for liquor and wine products. The liquor stores[209] earned $160 million in profits in 2016.

The New Hampshire state and local governments operate many programs. These programs should fund themselves by simply charging a fee for their usage. This is the basic premise of tolls. If the government wants our money for a service or product, they should play fairly like the rest of society does. They should earn our money. If the government did not steal (property/education) taxes from you, would you voluntarily pay the same amount to send your children to government schools as you would for private schools? I could assume your answer. And that is precisely my point. We all have to earn our money fairly. Why should politicians get away with using monopolies, extortion, and mafia tactics to make their money?

Bonds

The D.C. Empire, state governments, and local governments ask for loans from citizens, much like citizens ask for loans from banks. Governments do this by selling bonds.[210] When a government needs money for a project, they borrow money from individuals for a set interest rate. They do this by selling a bond to anyone willing to buy it. The bond has a set timeline and a set interest rate. The bondholder receives regular interest payments and gets his loan (also referred to as his principal investment) back when the bond matures. The government gets a loan (without coercion) and the citizen lender gets a predictable interest rate on his investment. Everyone wins and nobody is coerced (other than the future generations who may be extorted by politicians who need money to pay off the bonds). Why couldn't bonds totally fund all government budgets? If people believe in the government's projects or simply want to support them, they would happily loan them the money. If so few people have enough faith in the politicians to loan them money for the project, they have no business spending money on such an unpopular endeavor.

Advertising

In addition to all the charity that is given by New Hampshire residents, at least three societal functions within my state are currently funded voluntarily.

In partnership with the New Hampshire Department of Transportation, the Adopt-A-Highway[211] and Sponsor-A-Highway programs maintain highways using volunteers and funds generated via advertising. Simply put, businesses pay a set fee per month or supply volunteers for cleanup in exchange for their company's name being displayed on a sign along the highway. The business receives advertising, the highway remains clean, and nobody is robbed of their hard-earned money.

Currently, businesses including Subway, McDonald's, Dunkin Donuts, IHOP, Denny's, Whole Foods, Weight Watchers, AAA, Hampton Inn, and Waste Management voluntarily do business with Adopt-A-Highway in exchange for advertising. Evidently, these businesses see value in this exchange. If they did not want to spend money on the program, they wouldn't. Nobody is forcing them to!

When we voluntarily transfer our money to another party, we are inherently asserting that we see more value in the product or service we receive than in the money we pay for it. When you spend a dollar on a coffee, you are essentially telling the cashier that you want the coffee more than you want that dollar bill. When one party uses violence or threats, this consensual arrangement becomes distorted and is no longer moral.

Cleverly utilizing buses,[212] bus stops, and their websites[213] as space for advertising, the Nashua and Manchester transit authorities receive money from businesses that want to place their advertisements in front of thousands of commuters. The Manchester city government encourages businesses to Adopt A Site[214] in the city, as well. In New York, the MTA[215] makes hundreds of millions[216] of dollars per year by leasing out prime real estate on their buses and subways to advertisers.

A Manchester ad-wrapped bus parks in front of the Hooksett Walmart in New Hampshire to unload passengers

Companies spend nearly 200 billion[217] dollars per year on advertising in the united states. Why wouldn't governments want to receive their fair share of that gold mine? If that isn't enough incentive, maybe abolishing mandatory, unethical, and inherently violent taxation could encourage politicians to step into the future of revenue generation.

Governments could take the concept of advertising a step further, though. Utilizing the same revenue model as millions of YouTube creators, podcasters, and talk-show hosts, they could sell ads in a multitude of ways. If they allowed a video streaming platform to host House and Senate sessions and hearings every day, the federal government could probably earn billions of dollars a year in ad revenue due to the millions of views such videos would garner. If a child reviewing toys on YouTube could earn $22 million a year[218] from ad revenue, I'm sure the D.C. Empire, a collection of the 600 (more like a few million) most brilliant people on Earth could easily generate a few trillion dollars a year. Keep in mind that the annual budget for the entire federal government is only around $5 trillion a year. If our leaders made a real attempt—or if they were forced to—they could surely replace taxation with passive income from ads.

Before you call me crazy for mentioning the idea of a government monetizing their videos by allowing the platform to serve ads to viewers before the video begins . . . what would you say if I told you that the New Hampshire government is currently doing exactly that (possibly due to my incessant pleas for them to do so)?

At least some videos posted by the "NH House of Representatives Committee Streaming" channel are monetized and serve ads. I know this for certain, because I am forced to watch at least five seconds of an advertisement before I can watch some of their videos.[219]

Get this book! Well, you already have it. So . . . tell a friend to get this book!!

One small example of how easy it would be to maintain roads in the absence of taxation and central planning comes from Domino's Pizza. On June 11th, 2018, Yahoo Finance[220] reported that Domino's Pizza had begun to fill potholes and repave roads. Yes, you read that right. It seems that Domino's has become totally fed up with its drivers and customers having their fresh pizza ruined by being bounced around vehicles due to potholes and terrible roads. Many politicians have failed for decades to fix their roads despite increasing taxes and receiving billions in federal DOT grants. Yet, many people are afraid of the notion of decreasing government taxation & spending, asking *"who would build the roads?"* in the absence of mandatory taxation, central planning by politicians, and government-paving contracts.

Let's compare the new Domino's road repair efforts with traditional road repair efforts:

Efficiency: The "greatest city" in the union spends around $300,000,000 per year on road repair and around a billion dollars each year for its entire DOT budget. Despite this, many NYC roads are so mangled that they can no longer be considered "flat." These roads regularly pop tires and break axles on cars. Fixing roads in NYC and all across the union can take months, years, or even decades. More often, though, they are never repaired. Politicians perpetually manage to increase taxes with 'road repairs' as their perpetual justification, though. In 2015, Vox[221] reported that President Obama requested a massive increase in federal spending of taxpayer dollars in order to fix roads and bridges. That figure? Less than $500 billion. The American Society of Civil Engineers said that the repairs would cost $1.6 trillion. President Trump ran on a similar platform and proposed a $1.7 trillion[222] plan. This would cost every taxpayer around $15,000 dollars.

By contrast, Domino's does not benefit from inefficiency. In fact, they benefit from completing tasks while using the least amount of money and time possible. Since they are spending their own money, they use it wisely. They have begun repairing roads in four cities so far. In Milford, Delaware, the pizza franchise repaired 10 roads and 40 potholes—a feat that might cost millions and require thousands of man-hours when managed by government officials using taxpayer dollars—with only 4 workers in 10 hours, according to their website.[223]

Morality: Not only does Domino's Pizza repair roads much more efficiently than governments ever could, but they are doing it without using extortion. People have long been convinced by the government that roads could only ever be managed by politicians via central planning and funded by mandatory taxation. Keep in mind that if you don't pay your taxes, men with guns will come to your home and they will not leave without the money or your body. That makes taxation pretty mandatory . . . which makes it tantamount to extortion or armed robbery. Domino's is repairing roads without forcing any individuals to pay for them. They figure that fixing roads will benefit them by ensuring that pizzas arrive at their destinations intact and by supplying them with an incredible amount of good publicity. In fact, I would venture to say that the advertising benefit of their logo being placed on top of each repaired pothole (or strategically placed along the road if they were to advance into the business of primary road paving) would offset the cost of the road repairs. Domino's is now asking those who suffer from horrible government mismanagement of roads to nominate their town to be the next beneficiary of the new program.

Settle it in the ring

As I often explain, politics is often similar to professional wrestling entertainment. Two parties pretend to hate each other in order to put on a good show, while being friends with lots in common in real life. Well, what if the actual citizens could benefit from politicians fighting? Years ago, I half-jokingly proposed to box a Libertarian legislator in my home state of New Hampshire who happened to also be a boxer. I asked him how he'd feel about a boxing match that would raise money for a charity and/or the state government. Unfortunately, it never came to fruition. Others have toyed with the idea of allowing legislators to settle their disputes in a boxing ring. This idea could raise money for the government without stealing from citizens, it could bring the legislators closer together, and it could motivate them to lead much healthier lifestyles (boxers need to work out intensely for hours each day and they must eat extremely well). It's a fantastic proposition. And it wouldn't be totally groundbreaking.

All over the world, people are stepping into the ring to compete in a physical battle while raising money for charity. In 2021, two British friends raised £20,000[224] for charity in honor of their friend who passed away. In 2022, a practicing doctor raised $125,000[225] for the Boys and Girls Club of Harlem[226] in a single boxing match. Long Island Fight For Charity[227] has raised over $1.7 million for various charities. White Collar Boxing London[228] has raised over 2 million pounds for charities chosen by the fighters. If the British can do it, why can't we?

Actually, organizers of amateur combat sports events often direct all revenue from ticket sales to charity. In New Hampshire, this is actually the norm, possibly because the state government[229] waives the fees if the proceeds go to a charitable nonprofits. When I fought in my first boxing match[230] (an unofficial smoker) in 2019, all of the revenue from ticket sales went to charity. I would be happy to fight again for a good cause.

The more extreme the hostilities between politicians, the more attention the bout would garner. And as we discussed earlier, attention directly translates to revenue. Government officials who want to demonstrate their dedication to their constituents by utilizing creative ways to generate revenue for the government without robbing citizens using the threat of violence could earn money in a number of ways. The fight could have general admission and ringside tickets, the event could be pay-per-view, the video streaming platform could have commercials, the TV broadcast could have commercials, the venue could have advertisements, and the fighters could have sponsors on their shorts and other gear. By using one or more of the above revenue types, New Hampshire's 400 State Representatives (or thousands of government employees) could likely raise a large portion of the state's $6 billion annual budget.

In order to ensure that these amateur fighters remained relatively safe from serious injuries, they should consult with their doctors before fighting. They would also likely use 16-ounce gloves, which have much more padding than the gloves used by professional and amateur boxers.

Crowd-funding

If the majority of people really do support government programs, projects, and services as much as statists claim, then the majority of people would happily pay for them voluntarily. For instance, if local politicians wish to renovate the town hall, they should solicit funding from the people in the community who support the idea. This may sound similar to taxation, and it is—except that those who do not want those projects will not be forced at gunpoint to pay for them. If people can crowdfund millions[231] of dollars for ridiculous expenses, surely, the geniuses in government can use the same method to raise some money for the most useful and amazing projects, couldn't they?

Licensing

The federal government and state governments are capable of earning billions of dollars by leasing their licenses, trademarks, and patents to private firms. When a company wishes to use the NASA logo on its shirts, toys, or other products, it must pay the federal government money in exchange for permission to use its intellectual property. If a few companies each pay a few government agencies a small sum either monthly or based on sales (royalties), the government may be able to earn a substantial amount of money via this novel and peaceful method.

The D.C. Empire currently consists of over 400 agencies. They each have at least one logo. Many of them also hold various patents and licenses. Sticking with the NASA example, according to its official government website:[232] *"NASA owns over 1,000 patents and patent applications that protect inventions in hundreds of different subject matter categories. NASA makes these inventions available to industry through its Patent Licensing Program, which is administered by the NASA Office of the General Counsel, NASA Headquarters, Washington, D.C."*

As explained by UpCounsel.com:[233] *"Government-owned patents exist on inventions that have come from government-funded research. This type of research can exist in all types of industries among federal contractors, universities, corporations, small businesses, and research institutes. The government owns research facilities and provides research grants and procurement contracts to businesses in the private sector. Through these endeavors, the federal government provides funding for nearly half of the research and development efforts on a national scale, and because of its major investment, the government has the highest number of patent rights[234] in the country."*

While the federal government has historically allowed private firms to use its patents, it has been moving towards asserting its patent rights in recent years. As explained in the *NYU Law School Journal of Intellectual Property & Entertainment Law:*[235]

"In November 2019, HHS and the Department of Justice brought a patent infringement lawsuit against the drug company Gilead alleging infringement of government-owned patents on HIV prevention (HIV PrEP) and seeking potentially billions of dollars in damages."

As explained by CommonDreams.org[236]: *"...Pfizer's partner BioNTech has licensed[237] the [COVID vaccine] technology from the U.S. government and is paying royalties..."*

Personally, I would love to see the government gangsters be stripped of their power to initiate force. The enforcement of "intellectual property" law by the government is also dubious in the eyes of many libertarians and voluntaryists. However, if the government's workers really do create amazing new inventions and assert their patent claims, I would much rather see the government earn money from licensing agreements (*a priori*) than from patent infringement lawsuits (*post factum*). This is yet another method that governments could employ if they wish to earn revenue by non-violent means.

Taking into account all the aforementioned revenue-generating methods, politicians may be able to earn enough money to run the government without cutting spending. They might even have a surplus, which could be given to the truly needy or to those who have been forced to pay a quarter of their salary to the government every year for decades. As we've learned from billboards and government ad sales, any space that is visible to the public can be leased to advertisers for substantial amounts of money. Why are the inner and outer walls of every capitol building plain white? Why aren't they generating passive income[238] for the government? Could you imagine how much money Musk or Bezos would pay each year to advertise on such prime real estate?? The government could put every square inch of its property up for bid and raise billions or trillions of dollars without taxation and without violating anyone's consent!

"That's great, Alu. But the New Hampshire state budget is like six billion dollars per year. The NH government could never raise that much money without taxation!" one might argue.

A few rebuttals, if I may:

First, nothing justifies theft or extortion. A "6-billion-dollar budget" is a really bad excuse for the violation of property rights. If you are not earning enough money, is the solution to a) minimize expenses, b) improve your products/services, or c) use violence to obtain more money?

I think that the first and second options are great, and are often appropriate. I do not like the violent option, though. Shouldn't the government be held to the same moral standards that all humans are?

The Manchester Police Dept. currently uses this concept of ads/donations to fund their mounted unit

Second, the budget could easily be trimmed by a few billion dollars if politicians would stop promising to redistribute (an ever-increasing amount of) our hard-earned money to those who choose not to work. In my home state of New Hampshire, it could be trimmed by another $1.5 billion if politicians stopped funding government schools (don't worry, local governments throughout the state still spend $3 billion per year on their schools). Ending the forcible redistribution of wealth (welfare) would shave another $500 million per year from the state budget.

Third, the government could reasonably raise $6 billion per year by utilizing and expanding upon the methods outlined herein. I would estimate that if competent people were in charge, they could raise $10 billion.

Fourth, if the citizens felt that politicians were appropriately using the money they did have, they would donate to the government when they felt it was necessary. If these methods of revenue generation were to fall short of the necessary budget, there is nothing stopping New Hampshire residents (who happen to be the highest-earning people in the union) from voluntarily writing a check to the state government to bridge the fiscal gap!

In addition to their massive federal income tax burden, the average resident of New Hampshire pays around $5,000 per year in property taxes. If you've ever been furious about being forced to pay $600 to register[239] your vehicle before being allowed to drive it (on the very roads that you paid for with other taxes) or if you've wondered why we are forced to pay $5,000 per year for the privilege or living in the house that you bought, I implore you to consider that the New Hampshire government could raise enough money to fund their state budget (which seems to be around $6 billion per year, presently) without taking money from anyone by force. Indeed, the government can generate revenue without the violent act of coercion or extortion—it already does!

Regardless of whether your justification for mandatory extortion was that it stemmed from necessity or whether you believed that we were truly represented by the current voting system, any defense of extortion is illegitimate. Politicians do not represent us. Taxation is not moral. Taxation is not necessary. We now have the 21st-century solution to funding the government and other providers of necessary services. It is time to stand up to the corrupt, immoral thugs who extort our money to enrich themselves. It is time to start respecting property rights. It is time to condemn all violence and theft. It is time for a truly peaceful society.

**WITHOUT GOVERNMENT,
WHO WOULD PROVIDE _______ ?**

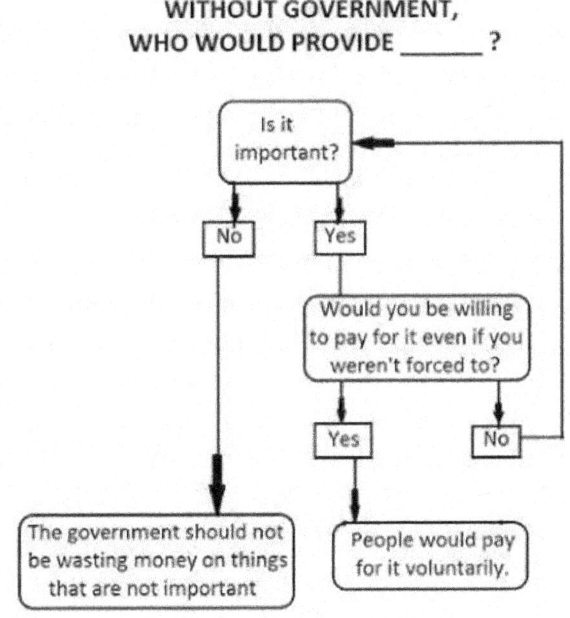

Chapter 11: Why Does The Government Exist?

Why did our ancestors even create governments?

In response to the overbearing British government, the colonists drafted a formal Declaration of Independence[240] and delivered it to their government. The document explained that governments ought to serve a primary purpose of protecting individual freedom, not violating it:

"When in the Course of human events, it becomes necessary for one people to dissolve the political bands which have connected them with another, and to assume among the powers of the earth, the separate and equal station to which the Laws of Nature and of Nature's God entitle them, a decent respect to the opinions of mankind requires that they should declare the causes which impel them to the separation. We hold these truths to be self-evident, that all men are created equal, that they are endowed by their Creator with certain unalienable Rights, that among these are Life, Liberty, and the pursuit of Happiness. That to secure these rights, Governments are instituted among Men, deriving their just powers from the consent of the governed, –That whenever any Form of Government becomes destructive of these ends, it is the Right of the People to alter or to abolish it, and to institute new Government, laying its foundation on such principles and organizing its powers in such form, as to them shall seem most likely to effect their Safety and Happiness."

Of course, this document speaks for itself. It simply explains that individuals who believe in freedom ought to take it upon themselves to leave their authoritarian rulers. Let's break down the key parts of the Declaration's first two paragraphs to help explain this point even more clearly, though:

"...to dissolve the political bands..."

This phrase clearly indicates that independence from rulers is absolutely moral, legal, and often a necessary defense against an abusive government.

"...which impel them to the separation..."

Again, this phrase indicates total support for secession by the very men who created this government. Massive historical evidence further proves[241] that the founders supported leaving governments that do not serve the people.

"...We hold these truths to be self-evident..."

The founders considered it 'self-evident' that every person knew right from wrong and liberty from tyranny. When I'm feeling optimistic, I believe that every individual must believe that they own themselves and that they aren't government property. But far too often, I feel like many people have been so thoroughly conditioned and brainwashed that they believe that politicians in the government rightfully own them.

"...that all men are created equal..."

Of course, modern politicians are considered lords while we serfs are abused increasingly every day. This is very far from the relationship that our founders envisioned for citizens and political leaders.

"...certain unalienable Rights..."

The founders are referring to natural human rights, which could never be taken away from any individual, no matter what. Rights cannot be revoked, even if 99% or 51% or 48% or 3% voted to strip a person of those natural rights. Even if a person is a minor or a felon. These rights include the right to property, the right to self-defense, and the right to pursue happiness.

"...to secure these rights..."

The government was created for the primary purpose of **protecting** our natural rights, also known as 'unalienable rights' and 'natural freedoms'.

"...consent of the governed..."

Notice that it does not say *"...consent of the majority of the governed..."*, nor does it say *"...consent of the plurality of the governed."* Therefore, we must assume that the founders created the federal government with the premise that a government could only legitimately exist and govern a group of individuals in a nation with support from each individual. Of course, few people actually consent to being governed by D.C. politicians, and nearly all of them[242] despise the federal government. A recent poll found that only 23%[243] of Americans think that the united states are headed in the right direction. Another recent poll found that only 7%[244] have a great deal of faith in Congress. Congressmen and presidents rarely ever get even half of the registered voters to support them. Keep in mind that President Trump was elected with the support of less than 26% of eligible voters. Think about that. Less than a fifth of the individuals in the union voted for someone, and that man is now our king. Due to the government thugs no longer possessing the 'consent of the governed', they no longer comprise a legitimate government. Arguing otherwise would indicate that you support mob rule.

"...it is the Right of the People to alter or to abolish it..."

This phrase is very clear and does not need much explanation. The founders strongly supported abolishing unjust governments by any means necessary, including by revolution.

While some might argue that the current federal Government does not consider the Declaration of Independence to have any legal authority, it is impossible to argue against this fact: if not for the Declaration, the federal government—and the Constitution that created it—would never have come to exist. Before creating a new government, ties to the previous one first had to be severed. Without acknowledging the legitimacy of the Declaration of Independence, one cannot believe the Constitution to be legitimate. Without a legitimate divorce, one cannot remarry.

Responsible Americans ought to consider the advice of our forefathers as we seek refuge from an increasingly abusive authoritarian regime. Americans are becoming quite open to various forms of independence from D.C. politicians. If the founders were alive, they would surely support abolishing or leaving the D.C. Empire over the perpetual cycle of increasing abuses against Americans by politicians and increased laws and taxes created by those same politicians under the guise of 'helping the needy'. If you hired a bodyguard to protect you, and all he did was stab you and kick you in the face and rob you instead of protecting you, you would fire him. If you held an investment property for revenue purposes and it drained your bank account instead of growing it, you would eventually get rid of it. If you paid a doctor to make you feel better and he consistently made you sicker, you'd eventually look for another doctor. If something has a primary purpose and consistently fails to serve that purpose, it should be discarded. It is indisputable that the federal government was created for the primary purpose of protecting our individual liberties. Being that the D.C. Empire does not protect those freedoms—and is the greatest threat to those freedoms—it no longer serves its purpose. If you believe in the Declaration of Independence, you should believe in the dissolution of the federal government. At the very least, you should support cutting ties with D.C. politicians and supporting state independence.

The Constitution sought to create a limited government.

That government has grown into one of the largest empires the world has ever seen. Can we finally admit that the experiment failed miserably?

If its primary mission is not to protect our rights, why does the federal government exist? It is obvious that the government violates our rights and liberties more than it protects them. A recent SurveyUSA poll[245] found that 65% of New Hampshire voters believe that D.C. politicians violate our rights more than they protect our rights, while only 27% believed the opposite to be true.

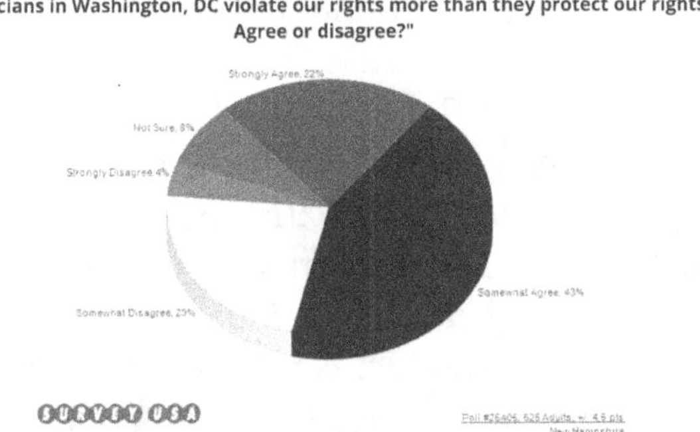

Occam's Razor is the principle of simplicity; the simplest answer requiring the least complicated explanation is most likely the correct one. Being that humans who possess power naturally desire to maintain and expand their power, this could be the simplest explanation for the existence of the government and the behavior of politicians.

Politicians control the citizenry by utilizing many forms of compulsion, ranging from soft brainwashing to hardcore coercion. It is no secret that those in government are extremely closely related (marriage, siblings, etc.) to the most powerful players in media, education, entertainment, and every other influential institution. They use this network of public-private partnerships to keep us all under control. When all else fails, the government uses brute force —men with guns called "law enforcement" to enforce their laws and keep the citizenry in compliance.

Entire books could surely be written on the subject of retaining power. Suffice it to say that modern politicians are quite expedient in ensuring that they win reelection or alternately retaining power in the "private sector" in media or enterprise if they can't remain in office.

As for the expansion of their powers, politicians accomplish this by constantly taking freedom and resources away from their subjects. When held by citizens, it's called "freedom." When held by government agents, it's called "power." And it is zero-sum. As we lose individual freedom, politicians necessarily gain power. Like businesses, governments constantly seek to grow; they hate stagnation and strive for exclusivity and utter dominance in their field. Businesses use voluntary interactions to gain money from willing customers. Governments use force to seize power from citizens.

Just how much have politicians enriched themselves by using "government" to their advantage?

Powerful politicians like Clinton, Biden,[246] Kerry, and many others cut deals with the world's most vicious dictators to enrich themselves. Of course, they often funnel the billions of dollars they receive through 'foundations' or family members, because they are not scrutinized by federal law, unlike the politicians themselves. But anyone with a brain could easily connect the dots.

In a nutshell, their scheme often looks something like this: a major political player (Xi Jinping, Vladimir Putin, etc.) wants access to the D.C. Empire or approval for a major international project, so they send massive amounts of money to the politician via a "pass-through" entity such as a relative, friend, or "charity," and then the project is approved and the politician is enriched. Because American politicians offer billions of dollars stolen from taxpayers each year to nearly every country on Earth, they use that money to extort foreign leaders. When the Ukrainian prosecutor was investigating Vice President Biden's son for corruption, Biden threatened to withhold $500 million in taxpayer money to the Ukrainian government if they did not fire the prosecutor. It worked. And Biden boasted about this flagrant extortion[247] at a live event on camera shortly afterward.

Socialist politician Michael Bloomberg has a net worth of around $60 billion. Many politicians have used their positions in government to earn money via bribes and other corrupt deals. Even in the cases where their wealth is not built via illegal corruption, they use their notoriety granted by their government position to earn millions. One such example was Obama's lucrative advance payment on his book after leaving the White House in 2017.

As President, Obama gave Pearson Publishing $350 million to create Common Core text. To return the favor, Pearson gave Obama a $65 million book deal in return, as noted by Investment Watch.[248]

After using his position as Dictator of New York to eliminate massive amounts of liberty for citizens, mishandling the coronavirus pandemic terribly, and then lying about how many seniors he killed by bringing the virus into nursing homes, Andrew Cuomo landed a $5 million[249] book deal, thanks to his position as Dictator. Ironically, the book was about how brilliantly he handled the scamdemic of corona-fascism.

Anthony Fauci, the most powerful man in the world since 2020, is paid over $400,000[250] per year by taxpayers. He also could make billions over the next few years in speaking fees and book deals, thanks to his position in government. As far as politicians, bureaucrats, and law enforcers are concerned, the main reason for the government to exist is to ensure that the members of their gang maintain and grow their power over the filthy peasants. Of course, they will continue to insist that they are there to "serve" us and to "protect" us from those who wish to harm us or violate our rights. But don't be fooled; politicians serve themselves and not their citizens. And they do not protect us or our rights, because the greatest threat to our rights always has been and always will be the government itself. How could it simultaneously be our protector and our greatest abuser?

Chapter 12: Where We Go From Here

We have now established with powerful evidence and logic that taxation is both immoral and unnecessary. Now what?

If I have successfully convinced you that "legalized extortion" should be abolished if we are to consider ourselves civilized sentient beings, then we must figure out how to practically make this a reality so that our children and grandchildren can live in a truly peaceful world where no extortion is considered legal.

According to a survey of over 200,000 Americans from 2018-2023, Civiqs.com[251] found that 59% support raising taxes on the wealthy while only 31% oppose the idea. Less than a third of the people in the union oppose tax increases. Almost two thirds support raising taxes. If you want lower taxes, you are in the minority.

We can eliminate the largest tax by simply leaving the D.C. Empire. I do not mean that you should move; most foreign nations have almost as much taxation and tyranny as the Empire. I mean that you should begin efforts to withdraw your state from the union. If you live in a state where this seems impossible, move to a state where liberty is more popular and independence more likely. Currently, Texas seems to have the most patriotic (loyal to Texas, not to DC) citizenry. After Texas, California is likely the second most patriotic state. The most libertarian states (Wyoming, New Hampshire, Florida) seem to have quite a lot of state pride, though the mountain west states seem to have very proud citizens, as well.

Of course, all 50 states in the union were once independent countries or territories, self-governing nations, just like Germany, France, and Britain were completely independent before joining the European Union. As you may already be aware, Britain did accomplish the unthinkable when its citizens voted to withdraw[252] from the European Union in 2016, a feat that left this author with his foot in his mouth. Actually, around a hundred other states around the world have declared independence from larger nations or unions over the past few decades. So, secession and independence may not be quite as far-fetched an idea as the media, politicians, and government-run schools have led us to believe.

Still, educated citizens in many pro-freedom states do have a lot of pride in their states. People in Wyoming often fly their state flag and most of them seem to despise everyone in DC. In New Hampshire, the state flag and motto can be found all over, including on shirts, signs, bags, and much more. Other than a few progressive areas, most of the states do seem to have a lot of citizens who take great pride in their individual state identities.

Every state likely has at least a small independence movement. Texas recently saw six state representatives sponsor a bill that sought to place the question of independence on the ballot for the people to vote on. Recent Texas polls found that 66% of its citizens[253] support independence. The Texas Republican Party officially placed "Texit" into their platform after 90% of the delegates[254] to their convention voted in favor of secession. Nine legislators in New Hampshire proposed legislation[255] to place independence on the ballot. All but 13 Representatives cowered and voted against the measure due to threats of treason charges. In August 2022, the state's Ballot Law Commission unanimously dismissed[256] the official complaint to remove the secessionists from the ballot, allowing them to run for reelection. This dismissal may empower dozens more legislators to vote for independence without fear of being charged with treason. The New Hampshire independence[257] movement is strong and growing more popular each day.

The past few years have seen millions of Americans self-segregating by moving to states that more closely align with their values. Many conservatives and libertarians have left California and New York and moved to Florida, Texas, Tennessee, and New Hampshire. The 2020 census[258] underscores the reality that the union is growing more polarized by the day; some states are becoming more pro-freedom while other states are becoming more authoritarian. Eventually, the states will separate from one another, meaning that the union will be broken.

While a state leaving the united states may seem extremely difficult at the moment, the polarization has made it clear that disunion is inevitable. Either states will leave the union or the D.C. Empire will totally collapse. Once a state is no longer officially in the united states, the federal income tax, the federal corporate tax, and all other federal taxes would immediately be eliminated for the state's citizens.

As for the practical process of secession, this could get a little tricky. In general, I would say that a critical mass of the state's citizens would have to demonstrate their support for independence. Ideally, the legislature and the governor would support the decision, and the people would overwhelmingly vote in favor of it on a ballot referendum. Hopefully, that would be enough for the federal government to recognize the declaration of independence, at least enough to refrain from attacking the state militarily.

A recent SurveyUSA poll found that only 6% of Americans would support military action against a state that declared independence from the union. As I mentioned in *The Blueprint For Liberty*,[259] even the D.C. Empire's military would have a difficult time killing massive amounts of New Hampshire citizens, because they would either have to go door to door or bomb entire cities, neither of which would be feasible.

Imagine that your state (I'll imagine that it's New Hampshire, personally) has left the union and that you can keep an extra 20% of your salary each year. Imagine that your employer is also saving millions per year, which allows them to spend more money on operations, salaries, bonuses, and expansion. Life would be much better, but we would still have state and local taxes. How could we abolish those?

Once the pathway between state and D.C. politicians (the career ladder) is severed, state lawmakers would immediately begin to behave differently; they would represent the will of their constituents much more responsibly. My father explained this concept in an excellent 2020 article titled "National Ambition Harms Constituents."[260]

Do national ambitions negatively affect state officials?

In the wonderful discussion we had with Daniel Miller, the President of the Texas Nationalist Movement on The Liberty Block's podcast,[261] every question posed to him was answered to my satisfaction. One of his assertions may not have received the attention it should have, though. Mr. Miller mentioned that almost all state politicians, whether Representatives, Senators, or even Governors, have "higher" ambitions, i.e., they all eventually want to be Congressmen, Senators, or the President of the D.C. Empire. Secession would take away this ambition, and with it, the negative influence this ambition has on the health of a state and the manner in which they govern.

As long as a politician seeks "higher" office, his eyes will not be primarily focused on the health and welfare of his own state or its citizens. It will almost always be tempered by thoughts such as *what will the national media say about me?* *what will the leaders of my Party think about me?* and *what will they think of me when I get to DC?*

Considering how difficult it is to attain national office without the help of Party leaders (financially and otherwise), it is not realistic to expect any politician to not always bear this in mind when considering any laws or issues in their own state. We have seen this in nearly 100% of cases, including among Republicans.

Chris Sununu, the Governor-turned-Dictator of New Hampshire, does not do what his constituents desire. Instead, he governs based on what he thinks will help him arrive and thrive in the U.S. Senate. Everyone in New Hampshire knows that he is likely to run for the U.S. Senate when he is finished playing Dictator. Governor Abbott of Texas does not govern with his eyes on Texas. He spends more time looking east toward DC; he wants to be there and will do whatever will please those in DC; regardless of how it affects Texans. The same is true for nearly all politicians throughout the union.

The growing D.C. Empire, which is infinitely larger than it was designed to be, has changed the relationship between state officials and their citizens. Other than this power somehow devolving back to the states, secession seems to be the only way to change this dynamic. This is not to say that secession does not have many more advantages for citizens of a state, just to point out how the changing dynamic between the federal government and those of individual states has made it almost impossible for state officials to concern themselves only with state issues. Simply put, if you want your state government to be most concerned with your state, you should support secession. Adding to this is the 17th Amendment, whereby concern with only one's state is no longer a promising path to being elected as a U.S. Senator by one's state and the reality is now totally different. At least when U.S. Senators were elected by state legislatures, loyalty to one's state would have been much greater.

So, secession would eliminate all federal taxes, and it would make the state lawmakers more accountable to the desires of their citizens. If the citizens wanted to abolish legalized theft, the newly-loyal state officials would be more likely to accommodate those wishes.

As discussed previously, the independent state could now begin to make taxation voluntary while simultaneously increasing its utilization of consensual revenue generation.

If you are tired of paying for armed men and women to pull you over for asinine infractions such as license plate lights being out, you should support making state and local taxation voluntary. Once you are no longer forced by the politicians to fund your own abuse at the hands of local cops, you could choose not to pay for over-aggressive policing. You could either save a lot of your earned income or you and your neighbors could meet with your police department and make your desires known. Once they truly have to satisfy their citizens, they will be forced to be more responsive to their desires. Essentially, voluntary taxation would create an opt-out clause in every governmental policy. If you do not want the service, simply cancel your subscription and stop paying for it. Currently, if I don't want to buy a lottery ticket, I don't buy one. If I do want an extra license plate, I pay for it. Simple as that!

The great thing about voluntary taxation is that pro-government citizens have no effective argument against it. If they love their government-run, taxpayer-funded schools, they can keep sending their children to them. Nobody will knock down their schools; some dissatisfied taxpayers may simply choose to stop funding an operation that they consider to be evil or ineffective. But those who do support the governmental education system can continue to pay for it and continue to enjoy its benefits. Not much would change for those people, to be honest. The same would be true of all other government programs, from social security to the fire department. Stealing money from people and justifying the theft by giving them a service they never requested and don't want does not absolve the thief of his crime.

I've heard many dissatisfied extortion victims (referred to as "taxpayers" by politicians) tell me that they have considered keeping all their money, but haven't done so due to the politicians' threats of punishment for failing to "pay taxes." These punishments could be severe and may include prison. From time to time, someone will mention that maybe we should all stop paying federal income taxes at the same time so that the politicians have no recourse. The IRS can't arrest or kill 165 million people if every worker in the union decided to stop allowing themselves to be extorted. Of course, a tax protest on a state level would be much more effective. For example, if 20,000 pro-liberty workers in New Hampshire refused to pay taxes, the 400 state troopers[262] could not arrest them all, and the courts could not process a fraction of them anyway. Additionally, a jury of libertarians would be unlikely to unanimously convict their neighbor for resisting extortion.

Of course, many people will remain unconvinced that they could or should stop allowing themselves to be extorted. In general, the acceptance of slavery or the unhealthy love of a slave towards their master or a victim towards their ongoing perpetrator is referred to as Stockholm Syndrome. Even if only a small fraction of individuals stopped paying federal income taxes—say, the 4.5 million people who voted Libertarian[263] in 2016—it might be enough to impair the federal government significantly and to allow the tax-evaders to avoid punishment.

Due to the brilliant policy in which employers 'withhold' federal income taxes from each employee's paycheck before the employee even sees the money, it would be quite difficult for most employed people to stop paying income taxes. Self-employed people could simply stop filing and paying taxes, though. Everyone else would have to ask their employers to give them their full paychecks without paying (payroll and) income taxes to the government. Just like it would be with individuals, solidarity among many large businesses might be the key to accomplishing this. If you are a business owner and you disagree with how federal politicians (people like Biden, Trump, Obama, Bush, Clinton, etc.) spend taxpayer dollars or if you simply oppose extortion, all you need to do is stop withholding money from your employees on behalf of the politicians.

Some believe that everyone who is tired of being abused and extorted (and abused again with the extorted money) should make a true new year's resolution at the end of this year:

"Beginning with my next paycheck, I will not allow politicians to extort me. I earned all of my money, and I intend to keep all of it!"

If federal politicians lost a trillion dollars or even a few hundred billion dollars in one year, politicians would be forced to make a difficult decision. They could concede and abolish the federal income tax, because once American workers realize that a few million workers are getting away with paying no taxes, it's only a matter of time before the rest of them stop allowing themselves to be extorted. The D.C. politicians could print more money, which would devalue the pathetic fiat dollar so much that it might finally collapse. This would hurt, but it would be an amazing win for freedom in the long run. They could try to borrow even more money from the Federal Reserve, which would hurt the government and the dollar. Or they could make the most rational and moral choice: radically cut spending. The government could easily cut a trillion dollars in spending without harming anyone. In fact, society would benefit immensely from keeping an additional trillion dollars (around $10,000 per worker) with which to buy houses, cars, or anything else they desire. And people throughout the union and the world would be much safer from the D.C. Empire's armed thugs. And the federal behemoth that has grown by leaps and bounds every year since 1789 would be shrunk for the first time in its history. Indeed, this would be the first significant win for liberty since the American revolution. Are you in?

Ultimately, my greatest wish is that individuals could be the true owners of all their property, including their money. Ideally, free men should have the power to decide how each penny is spent. The days of slavery are but distant memories of a despicable past. My hope is that government-perpetrated extortion will once be condemned in a similar manner by historians. At this very moment, you and I have an opportunity to abolish one of the last remaining barbaric customs practiced by a supposedly civilized society.

How can you begin to make a difference today?

Start calling taxation what it really is: Theft.

The End

Thank you very much for reading this book! If you have any questions about taxation or independence that were not answered, please reach out to alu.axelman@gmail.com.

Scan QR code to visit the book's page on Amazon

Endnotes

1. nps.gov/articles/000/sugar-and-stamp-acts.htm
2. hoover.org/research/colonial-roots-american-taxation-1607-1700
3. parliament.uk/about/living-heritage/transformingsociety/towncountry/towns/tyne-and-wear-case-study/about-the-group/housing/window-tax
4. fsp.org/pine-tree-riot-a-history-of-rebellion
5. britannica.com/event/Boston-Tea-Party
6. history.com/topics/american-revolution/american-revolution-history
7. thoughtco.com/constitutional-convention-105426
8. gilderlehrman.org/history-resources/spotlight-primary-source/brawl-between-federalists-and-anti-federalists-1788
9. libertyblock.com/the-constitution-vs-liberty
10. politico.com/story/2009/08/lincoln-imposes-first-federal-income-tax-aug-5-1861-025787
11. taxfoundation.org/today-history-income-tax-ruled-unconstitutional-pollock-v-farmers-loan-trust-co
12. energy.gov/eere/solar/homeowners-guide-federal-tax-credit-solar-photovoltaics
13. yahoo.com/lifestyle/the-government-wants-to-pay-people-for-having-kids-is-this-a-good-idea-155102268.html
14. federalreserve.gov/monetarypolicy/bst_fedsbalancesheet.htm
15. federalreserve.gov/data/intlsumm/current.htm
16. FSP.org
17. statista.com/statistics/1040079/life-expectancy-united-states-all-time
18. libertyblock.com/the-disgusting-war-against-ivermectin
19. newsmax.com/Health/Health-News/fda-red-tape-blocks/2014/08/21/id/590142
20. nasi.org/learn/social-security/retirement-age
21. money.usnews.com/money/retirement/social-security/articles/the-history-of-your-social-security-payments
22. libertyblock.com/taxes-on-taxes
23. ssa.gov/policy/docs/ssb/v46n7/v46n7p3.pdf
24. govinfo.gov/content/pkg/STATUTE-79/pdf/STATUTE-79-Pg286.pdf
25. medicare.gov/Pubs/pdf/10050-Medicare-and-You.pdf
26. whitehouse.gov/wp-content/uploads/2021/05/budget_fy22.pdf
27. cms.gov/newsroom/news-alert/cms-releases-latest-enrollment-figures-medicare-medicaid-and-childrens-health-insurance-program-chip
28. amzn.to/3K2452d
29. calculator.net/inflation-calculator.html?cstartingamount1=1&cinyear1=1971&coutyear1=2022&calctype=1&x=67&y=29
30. coincollectingenterprises.com/information/penny-facts/year-compositions
31. eidebailly.com/insights/articles/2020/4/federal-reserve-eliminates-reserve-requirements
32. cashmoneylife.com/us-mint-cease-penny-production
33. youtu.be/NJd6RKsY5H4
34. civiqs.com/results/track_country
35. pjmedia.com/vodkapundit/2021/06/10/covid-unemployment-fraud-hundreds-of-billions-of-your-tax-dollars-went-to-foreign-criminals-n1453536
36. libertyblock.com/is-taxation-outdated
37. dailytorch.com/2012/10/u-s-taxpayer-dollars-sent-to-foreign-countries-that-oppose-u-s-interests-aids-no-one

38. zerohedge.com/news/2016-01-02/isis-enemy-us-created-armed-funded
39. yahoo.com/nh-crossfit-gym-ordered-close-220214768.html
40. investopedia.com/terms/l/laffercurve.asp
41. youtu.be/FCk2-QVqCck
42. heritage.org/taxes/report/tax-cuts-increase-federal-revenues
43. libertyblock.com/evil-tyrants-try-to-trick-people-into-supporting-massive-new-t axes
44. wikipedia.org/wiki/United_states_federal_budget
45. msn.com/en-us/money/markets/the-rich-already-pay-too-much-in-taxes
46. taxfoundation.org/rich-pay-their-fair-share-of-taxes
47. nerdwallet.com/blog/taxes/dividend-tax-rate
48. smartasset.com/taxes/how-taxes-on-lottery-winnings-work
49. turbotax.intuit.com/tax-tips/jobs-and-career/how-bonuses-are-taxed
50. thebalance.com/how-is-the-gift-tax-calculated-3505674
51. taxfoundation.org/income-tax-code-spans-more-70000-pages
52. taxpolicycenter.org/briefing-book/what-are-major-federal-payroll-taxes-and-ho w-much-money-do-they-raise
53. taxfoundation.org/tanning-tax-two-weeks
54. libertyblock.com/nh-dems-lets-tax-the-ski-lift-tickets-too
55. finance.yahoo.com/news/the-democratic-plan-for-a-42-national-sales-tax-202 549219.html
56. investors.com/politics/commentary/cops-seize-more-in-assets-than-burglars-st eal-in-2014
57. boingboing.net/2020/12/21/us-police-have-stolen-68-billion-in-the-past-20-yea rs-from-american-citizens-without-due-process.html
58. washingtonpost.com/national-security/stephen-lara-nevada-asset-forfeiture-ad option/2021/09/01/6f170932-06ae-11ec-8c3f-3526f81b233b_story.html
59. heritage.org/research/reports/2014/03/civil-asset-forfeiture-7-things-you-shoul d-know
60. amzn.to/3aV9cnN
61. ij.org/press-release/lawsuit-uncovers-the-inside-story-of-the-fbis-plans-to-take-security-deposit-boxes-without-charging-owners-with-crimes
62. youtube.com/watch?v=AjTwcQYgISA
63. investopedia.com/insights/what-is-money
64. youtube.com/watch?v=wJVXonwWvPQ
65. youtu.be/lu_VqX6J93k?t=1800
66. youtube.com/watch?v=v0D1nVH1nX0
67. edge.app/blog/market-updates/formation-of-the-fed-the-meeting-at-jekyll-islan d
68. youtu.be/lu_VqX6J93k?t=2574
69. history.com/this-day-in-history/fdr-takes-united-states-off-gold-standard
70. data.bls.gov/cgi-bin/cpicalc.pl?cost1=100&year1=191301&year2=201810
71. thebalance.com/how-is-the-fed-monetizing-debt-3306126
72. newsweek.com/will-us-dollar-lose-its-place-worlds-no-1-reserve-currency-156 7224
73. msn.com/en-us/money/markets/minimum-wage-for-fast-food-workers-to-rise-i n-new-york-on-thursday/ar-AALDsvu
74. libertyblock.com/rebuttal-to-the-left-health-economy-healthy-people

75. federalreserve.gov/monetarypolicy/reservereq.htm
76. libertyblock.com/hey-nh-want-a-state-income-tax
77. docs.wixstatic.com/ugd/03ec84_0f2e1937feaf430c8ab5008b2ce8f076.pdf
78. libertyblock.com/does-hb628-create-an-income-tax-or-a-payroll-tax
79.capoliticalreview.com/trending/ca-senate-votes-28-8-to-exempt-itself-from-california-gun-laws
80. libertyblock.com/leftist-tactics-grouping
81.libertyblock.com/evil-tyrants-try-to-trick-people-into-supporting-massive-new-taxes
82.warren.senate.gov/imo/media/doc/Bill%20Text%20-%20Ultra-Millionaire%20Tax%20Act%20-%20March%201%202021.pdf
83. https://youtu.be/a2rJr7pntqQ
84.libertyviral.com/the-top-5-reasons-why-fdr-sucked-as-president/#axzz56B2BTzPK
85. libertyblock.com/the-freedom-to-invest
86.wyominggunowners.org/latest-news/nra-exposed-their-deadly-support-for-red-flag-gun-seizure-laws
87.nydailynews.com/news/politics/state-pols-mull-plan-add-750-speed-cameras-nyc-schools-article-1.3157608
88.nyc.streetsblog.org/2011/03/22/new-york-has-81875-metered-parking-spaces-and-millions-of-free-ones
89. newyorkparkingticket.com/nyc-parking-tickets-stats-facts
90. data.bls.gov/timeseries/LNS11300000
91.washingtontimes.com/news/2013/mar/28/food-stamp-president-enrollment-70-percent-under-o
92. libertyblock.com/the-empires-medical-system-is-becoming-disturbingly-racist
93.libertyblock.com/whites-are-bad-because-theyre-good-black-supremacists-claim
94. theblaze.com/slightly-offensve/anti-white-racism
95. mariettaoh9-12project.com/why-do-democrats-hate-families
96. wnd.com/2020/07/blm-leader-whites-subhuman-genetic-defects
97. nmaahc.si.edu/learn/talking-about-race/topics/whiteness
98. libertyblock.com/the-freedom-to-invest
99. washingtonpost.com/business/2021/09/03/social-security-insolvency
100. atf.gov/about-atf/budget-performance
101. justice.gov/jmd/page/file/1142431/download
102. epa.gov/planandbudget/budget
103.msn.com/en-us/news/money/american-taxpayer-dollars-funded-wuhan-lab-research-sen-ernst/vi-BB1gBCbh
104. libertyblock.com/rebuttal-to-the-left-health-economy-healthy-people
105. youtube.com/watch?v=9RK0HiMz3uA
106. www2.ed.gov/about/overview/budget/budget22/budget-highlights.pdf
107.thefederalist.com/2022/05/06/new-biden-title-ix-order-will-help-schools-push-transgenderism-on-your-kids-behind-your-back
108.startribune.com/junior-rotc-not-military-recruitment-but-quite-like-it
109. publicschoolreview.com/blog/why-82-of-public-schools-are-failing
110. visualcapitalist.com/u-s-military-personnel-deployments-country
111.militarytimes.com/veterans/2016/07/07/new-va-study-finds-20-veterans-commit-suicide-each-day
112. seniorcare.com/featured/aging-america

113. healthcare.gov/glossary/federal-poverty-level-FPL
114. rumble.com/virh6r-your-taxes-will-pay-for-this-mans-welfare.html
115. breitbart.com/national-security/2016/11/18/afghanistan-u-s-spending-taxpayer-funds-to-secure-85-million-abandoned-hotel-apartment-building
116. libertyblock.com/fda-cracks-down-on-diarrhea-medication
117. libertyblock.com/a-manchin-of-corruption
118. usa.gov/federal-agencies
119. westernjournal.com/powerful-weapons-armor-falling-hands-taliban-biden-beats-hasty-retreat
120. governing.com/columns/smart-mgmt/Big-Bucks-Buckle-Up.html
121. itstillruns.com/grants-police-vehicles-6922531.html
122. fosters.com/news/20171121/farmington-police-get-125000-federal-grant
123. huffpost.com/entry/police-tank-purchase-new-hampshire_n_1279983
124. fsp.org/bearcat
125. weaselzippers.us/203413-feds-fund-study-teaching-mountain-lions-how-to-ride-a-treadmill
126. tammybruce.com/2014/10/halloween-horror-feds-spend-44700-to-market-pumpkin-donuts-387000-to-massage-rabbits.html
127. media.defense.gov/2022/Oct/18/2003098052/-1/-1/1/UKRAINE-FACT-SHEET-OCT-14.PDF
128. nation.time.com/2012/10/02/the-mrap-brilliant-buy-or-billions-wasted
129. wired.com/2008/07/mrap-hazards-dr
130. kezi.com/content/national/498984691.html
131. fee.org/articles/the-f-35-project-has-been-a-disastrous-waste-of-money
132. investors.com/politics/editorials/obama-iran-terrorism
133. washingtontimes.com/news/2018/feb/7/inside-the-ring-obama-era-cash-traced-to-iran-back
134. libertyblock.com/covid-bill-redistributes-money-from-you-to-foreigners
135. bizpacreview.com/2020/12/22/10m-for-pakistan-gender-programs-america-first-trends-in-furious-response-to-pork-filled-covid-relief-bill-1008416
136. foreignassistance.gov
137. openthebooks.com/export-import-bank-2007-2021--openthebooks-oversight-report
138. washingtonexaminer.com/darrell-issa-irs-official-threw-government-contracts-to-a-friend
139. cbsnews.com/news/whitefish-energy-tiny-montana-company-awarded-huge-puerto-rico-contract-has-ties-to-trump-administration
140. vox.com/policy-and-politics/2017/11/15/16648924/puerto-rico-whitefish-contract-congress-investigation
141. cnbc.com/2021/04/14/companies-that-received-covid-government-contracts-under-trump-ramped-up-lobbying.html
142. propublica.org/article/trump-friends-and-family-cleared-for-millions-in-small-business-bailout
143. nypost.com/2020/09/23/hunter-biden-received-3-5m-from-russian-billionaire-report
144. foxnews.com/politics/hunter-biden-paid-80g-per-month-while-on-board-of-ukranian-gas-company-report
145. nypost.com/2022/01/27/chinese-elite-have-paid-some-31m-to-hunter-and-the-bidens

146.capoliticalreview.com/capoliticalnewsandviews/more-corruption-exposed-fro
m-the-biden-administration

147. oig.dhs.gov/sites/default/files/assets/2022-04/OIG-22-37-Apr22.pdf

148. judicialwatch.org/nonprofit-no-bid-contract-after-hiring-biden-official

149. bouncemojo.com/richest-politicians

150.dailyinterlake.com/news/2020/apr/19/rep-gianforte-responds-to-accusations-
about-6

151.dailymail.co.uk/news/article-8368021/Mike-Pences-chief-staff-holds-1-6m-sto
ck-firms-responding-pandemic.html

152. newsweek.com/stock-act-richard-burr-kelly-loeffler-1493497

153. libertyblock.com/the-non-representative-republic

154. ballotpedia.org/Jeanne_Shaheen

155.votesmart.org/candidate/key-votes/1663/jeanne-shaheen/37/guns#.Wz12Ud
JKiUl

156.votesmart.org/candidate/key-votes/1663/jeanne-shaheen/111/taxes#.Wz12h
NJKiUk

157. ballotpedia.org/Carol_Shea-Porter

158. ballotpedia.org/Chris_Christie_(New_Jersey)

159independent.co.uk/news/world/asia/kim-jong-un-wins-100-of-the-vote-in-north
-korean-elections-9180814.html

160. facebook.com/RepThomasMassie/videos/1905347912822697

161. youtube.com/watch?v=-QrKAaKHUi4

162. atr.org/nearly-4000-epa-regulations-issued-under-president-obama

163.encyclopedia.com/history/united-states-and-canada/us-history/food-and-drug
-act-1906

164.heritage.org/courts/report/who-will-regulate-the-regulators-administrative-age
ncies-the-separation-powers-and

165.washingtonpost.com/opinions/the-rise-of-the-fourth-branch-of-government/20
13/05/24/c7faaad0-c2ed-11e2-9fe2-6ee52d0eb7c1_story.html

166.freedomworks.org/content/obama%E2%80%99s-private-army-militarizing-fe
deral-agencies

167. youtube.com/watch?v=XFx19QU_ORs

168.uschamber.com/series/above-the-fold/the-riddle-how-agencies-can-make-so-
many-laws-easier-congress

169.nypost.com/2018/05/14/supreme-court-lifts-federal-ban-on-sports-betting

170.thehill.com/policy/finance/393441-supreme-court-rules-for-south-dakota-in-o
nline-sales-tax-case

171.reason.com/blog/2018/08/14/west-virginias-entire-supreme-court-just

172. supreme.justia.com/cases/federal/us/545/469

173. constitutioncenter.org/blog/felons-and-the-right-to-vote

174. youtube.com/watch?v=Mky11UJb9AY

175.unfccc.int/process-and-meetings/the-paris-agreement/the-paris-agreement

176. gunowners.org/n09252013.htm

177. youtube.com/watch?v=5tu32CCA_lg

178.breitbart.com/politics/2019/01/16/kobach-democrats-finally-acknowledge-that
-voter-fraud-exists

179.pbs.org/newshour/nation/an-11-year-old-changed-election-results-on-a-replic
a-florida-state-website-in-under-10-minutes

180.libertyblock.com/evidence-shows-voter-fraud-in-multiple-swing-states

181. youtu.be/DxlEtR1wZ1Q

182. hoover.org/research/colonial-roots-american-taxation-1607-1700
183. nber.org/system/files/working_papers/w22724/w22724.pdf
184. usa.gov/covid-stimulus-checks
185. libertyblock.com/sununu-tyrant-ironic-ubi-healthcare
186. data.worldbank.org/indicator/SL.TLF.TOTL.IN?locations=US
187. youtube.com/watch?v=IYO3tOqDISE
188. youtu.be/oDI_HHHbybA
189. youtube.com/channel/UC4a-Gbdw7vOaccHmFo40b9g
190. youtube.com/user/MEDCRAMvideos
191. youtube.com/channel/UCNI0qOojpkhsUtaQ4_2NUhQ
192. youtube.com/watch?v=2xSKCAtWIyo
193. forbes.com/sites/abrambrown/2022/01/14/the-highest-paid-youtube-stars-mr beast-jake-paul-and-markiplier-score-massive-paydays
194. adamenfroy.com/how-to-make-money-on-youtube
195. obuniversity.com/articles/how-i-made-a-million-dollars-in-the-outdoor-billboar d-business
196. new.mta.info/doing-business-with-us/advertising/opportunities
197. boredpanda.com/creative-ads-on-buildings/?utm_source=ecosia&utm_medi um=referral&utm_campaign=organic
198. libertyblock.com/pizza-the-key-to-road-repair
199. emarketer.com/content/emarketer-total-media-ad-spending-worldwide-will-ris e-7-4-in-2018
200. heritage.org/budget-and-spending/report/50-examples-government-waste
201. crsreports.congress.gov/product/pdf/R/R42346
202. statista.com/statistics/257364/top-lobbying-industries-in-the-us
203. maplight.org/story/foreign-lobbyists-contributed-more-than-4-5-million-to-can didates-in-2016-elections
204. commondreams.org/news/2016/02/22/most-democrats-prefer-socialism-capit alism
205. latimes.com/politics/la-na-pol-democrats-socialism-capitalism-20190320-stor y.html
206. youtube.com/watch?v=CzYN5CH4cvc
207. nhlottery.com/Where-The-Money-Goes.aspx
208. about.usps.com/newsroom/national-releases/2021/1110-usps-reports-fiscal-y ear-2021-results.htm
209. nhpr.org/post/nh-liquor-commission-touts-record-698m-sales-over-past-fiscal -year#stream/0
210. youtube.com/watch?v=IuyejHOGCro
211. adoptahighway.net/about-us
212. ataoutdoormedia.com
213. nashuanh.gov/485/Advertising
214. manchesternh.gov/Adopt-A-Site/Capital-Improvements
215. new.mta.info/doing-business-with-us/advertising/opportunities
216. new.mta.info/document/12481
217. statista.com/statistics/236958/advertising-spending-in-the-us
218. forbes.com/sites/jrose/2019/03/21/how-much-do-youtubers-really-make
219. youtu.be/TEiyC4vPrBs?t=12550
220. finance.yahoo.com/news/dominos-pizza-unveils-u-s-infrastructure-project-filli ng-potholes-130802630.html
221. vox.com/2015/2/10/8012211/infrastructure-crumbling-more-spending

222.https://www.businessinsider.com/trump-infrastructure-plan-in-state-of-the-uni
on-speech-text-2018-1
223. pavingforpizza.com/milford-de
224.derbytelegraph.co.uk/news/gallery/friends-raise-20000-beloved-derby-62867
57
225.nypost.com/2022/11/19/dr-mike-donates-125k-boxing-purse-to-harlem-youth
-organization
226. bgcharlem.org
227. lifightforcharity.org/about-us
228. whitecollarboxinglondon.com/charity
229. gencourt.state.nh.us/rsa/html/XXIV/285/285-13.htm
230. youtu.be/nUit_t2j6gl
231. mashable.com/article/gofundme-top-fundraisers-campaigns
232. nasa.gov/centers/stennis/ssc-partnerships/licensing-opportunities.html
233. upcounsel.com/government-owned-patents
234. upcounsel.com/patent-rights
235. jipel.law.nyu.edu/should-the-u-s-government-actively-assert-its-own-patents
236.commondreams.org/news/2021/04/23/nih-scientist-who-developed-key-vacci
ne-technology-says-patent-gives-us-leverage
237. keionline.org/35746
238. libertyblock.com/the-new-free-market-fund-anything-at-no-cost
239.manchesternh.gov/Departments/Tax-Collector/Motor-Vehicle-Registration/Ex
planation-of-Fees
240. archives.gov/founding-docs/declaration-transcript
241.libertyblock.com/kokesh-is-right-the-us-government-should-be-abolished
242.cbsnews.com/news/poll-congress-approval-rating-drops-to-11-percent
243.civiqs.com/results/track_country
244.news.gallup.com/poll/394283/confidence-institutions-down-average-new-low.
aspx
245.surveyusa.com/client/PollReport.aspx?g=f4ec3bab-2167-4e8e-ab64-671c1b
4a5ddd
246.breitbart.com/2020-election/2020/01/21/book-bombshell-james-bidens-firm-g
ot-1-5-billion-in-government-contracts-despite-zero-experience
247. youtu.be/Q0_AqpdwqK4?t=3128
248.investmentwatchblog.com/obama-gave-pearson-publishing-350-million-to-cr
eate-commoncore-text-and-pearson-gave-obama-a-65-million-dollar-book-deal-in
-return
249.nypost.com/2021/05/19/gov-cuomo-book-deal-leads-gop-to-demand-anti-cor
ruption-law
250.audacy.com/news/dr-anthony-fauci-is-our-highest-paid-federal-employee
251.civiqs.com/results/raise_taxes_wealthy
252. bcatoday.org/britain-votes-to-leave-e-u-cameron-to-step-down
253. tnm.me/news/political/bombshell-poll-66-of-texas-voters-want-texit
254.tnm.me/news/tnm-news/texas-republicans-call-for-texit-vote-with-90-in-favor
255.libertyblock.com/breaking-nh-legislator-submits-legislation-to-divorce-dc-decl
are-independence
256.libertyblock.com/dc-apologist-files-complaint-to-remove-pro-independence-re
ps-from-ballot
257. nhindependence.org
258. libertyblock.com/us-census-shows-how-people-vote-with-their-feet
259. amzn.to/3okuLRJ
260. libertyblock.com/national-ambition-harms-constituents
261.rumble.com/vcblml-the-ejs-podcast-on-the-liberty-block-episode-28.html
262. nhsp.dos.nh.gov/about-us
263. uselectionatlas.org/RESULTS/national.php